PACK UP AND PAINT

Flowers

Tom Robb

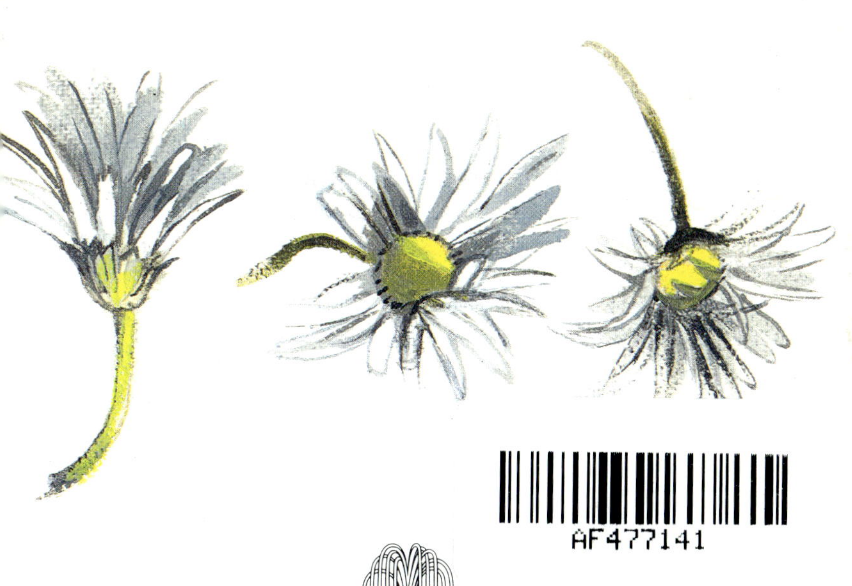

COLLINS

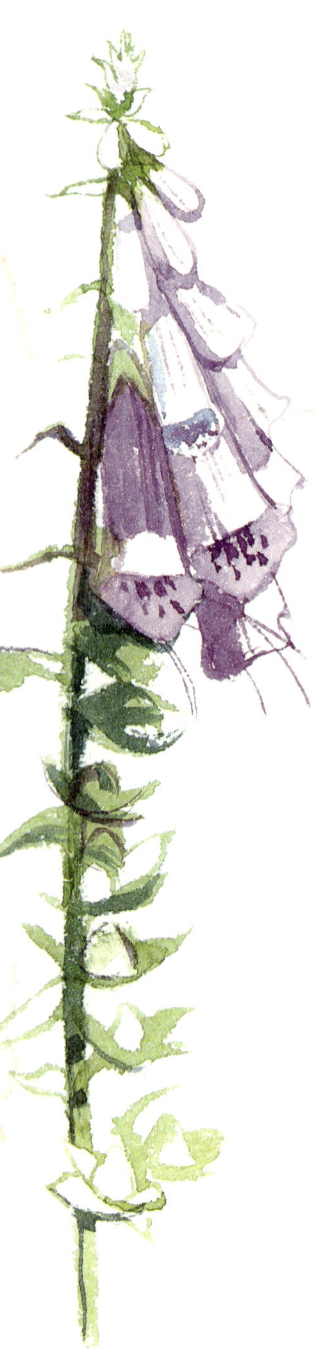

First published in 1987
by William Collins Sons & Co Ltd
London. Glasgow. Sydney
Auckland. Johannesburg

Designed and produced by
PHOEBE PHILLIPS EDITIONS

British Library Cataloguing in Publication Data

Robb, Tom
Pack up and paint flowers.
1. Flower painting and illustration
Technique
I. Title
751.4 ND1400

ISBN 0-00-412264-X

Printed and bound in Belgium by
Offset-Printing van den Bossche N.V.

Introduction

Flowers are about beauty, real beauty, in the same way that painting is about art. By appealing to our senses with incredibly complex shapes, graceful forms, delicious scents and an array of subtle and gaudy colours, flowers contribute to the quality of life at almost every level.

The botanical artist will find a miniature universe within the wheel of one daisy's petals. The impressionist can see the radiant light pouring from a field of poppies. The nature lover beams with pride and delight at the discovery of a species thought extinct but found flourishing on a remote hillside. The designer fills a dozen sketch-books, and suddenly the world is full of flower-based patterns.

But thinking about flowers as the major subject of a drawing or painting requires an entirely new attitude. One of the first adjustments you have to make is to the sense of scale – turning from a vista stretching miles into the distance towards a single curved stem no more than a foot or two in front of you. This change will reward you with an enhanced response to colour and detail. There is nothing more beautiful than the green leaves and whirl of colour we can find in any herb or buttercup.

Every outing to paint flowers has brought me greater appreciation and understanding. I hope some of the ideas and problems that I had to work through will help you to make the most of every minute out of doors, where the smallest scrap of flowered meadow becomes the painter's garden.

Tom Robb

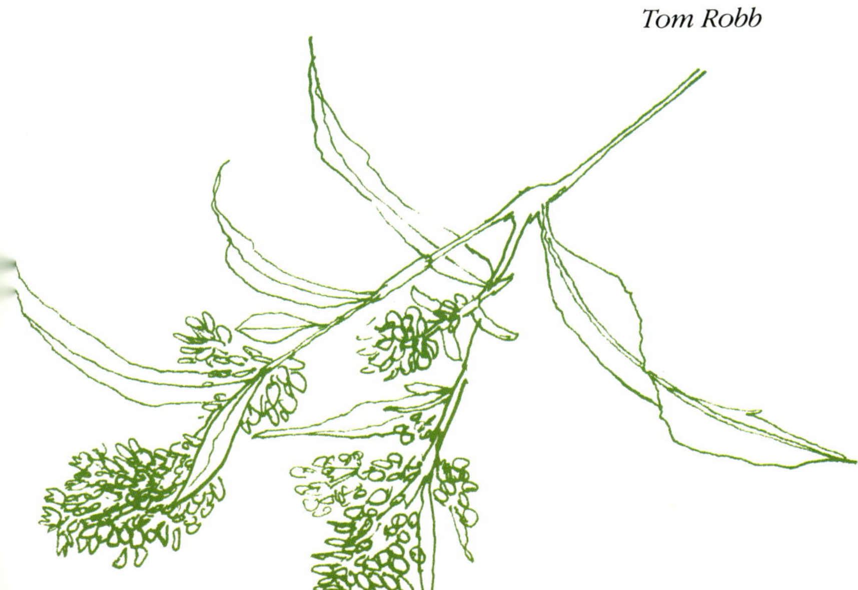

Contents

Why flowers?

Flowers have always been part of the landscapes that I enjoy so much, and even the oldest sketch-books that I still find tucked away underneath piles of canvases are crowded with drawings of petals, rose hips, and bramble hedges.

For once, the arts and the sciences meet in perfect accord. Conservation and the natural ecological balance depend upon how quickly we can learn to make painting part of life instead of an excuse for digging up a plant or cutting down a blossoming branch only to watch it gradually wither, pinned to a drawing board under artificial light.

Think of how much more you can discover out of doors. For anyone who simply wants a morning or a day of pleasure, a picnic expedition is perfect. Soak up colours and scents, collect a few berries or wild fruits and lay on pigments and washes with abandon.

Try this a second time, and you find that flowers become more individual – *and* more demanding, as well. A lick of green becomes a frond, a dash of colour, a petal. You'll begin to focus on the flower itself, on how it grows, what it needs to thrive, what it looks like when it's healthy or, perhaps, damaged in some way. You might become excited by the various yellows to be found on only one stem of golden rod, the purples in a single family of thistles, the textures of different rosebuds.

Finally, you can go beyond the boundaries set merely by observing flowers, to using them as a stimulus for your imagination, thus gaining a far richer and deeper appreciation of what you see.

Regardless of your level of experience, there are numerous complete worlds to be discovered in flower-painting, and they can exist for us all on different levels and at different times.

Make the most of your time out of doors; think about where you are going and what you want to achieve. And be prepared to ask yourself questions when you get back. Whichever the path you follow on any particular day, you'll soon see for yourself that there is nothing more pleasing to the eye than drawing and painting flowers – or more satisfying to the heart!

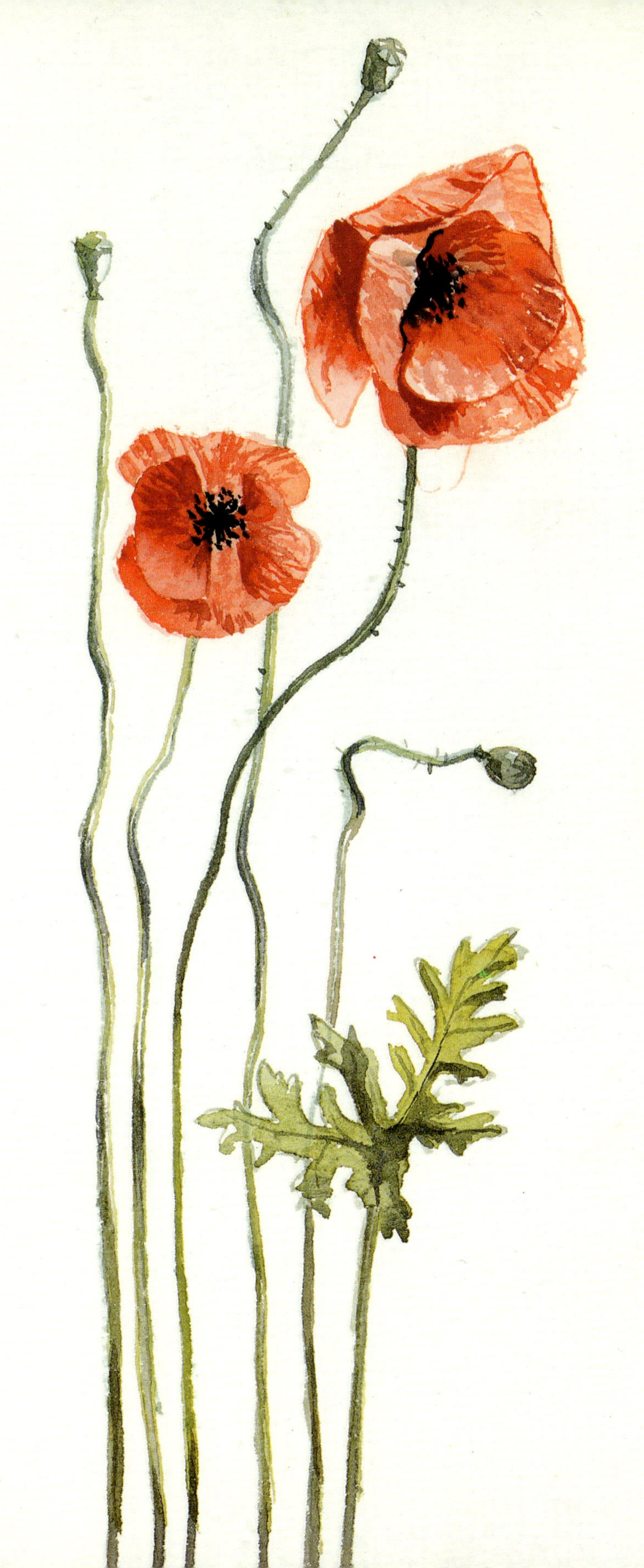

Practical planning

Going out to paint flowers can be a casual stroll, requiring nothing more than a handful of coloured pencils and a pad in your pocket. Or it can become a full-scale expedition high up in the mountains, in search of the remote home of a wild rambling rose.

What you will need

Equipment for your expedition naturally depends upon what medium you plan to use. But flowers have particular qualities that you must always take into account.

Working on a small scale requires precise tools. Although I usually love the varied textures and shadings of charcoal, I don't find it a particularly sympathetic medium for the intricacy of flower-painting. A big bouquet in a studio vase can be a fine subject for a marvellous smudgy drawing, but out of doors I prefer the control of pencils and pens.

Pencils should be sharp, giving a clean fine line, so use the harder numbers – any of the HB series. And don't forget the sharpener.

Felt-tip pens and coloured or plain inks are superb for capturing the detailed structures of flowerheads. Again – fine points, not heavy nibs.

Pastels convey the soft colours of many kinds of flower, but I use them more for longish views of flowering beds and meadows than for close-ups of individual clumps or blooms. Certainly the range of delicate shades makes it easy to find exactly the colour you want.

You must always protect your pastels in a hard case; otherwise you are likely to waste your money on a great deal of pretty dust. Oil pastels, like wax crayons, are a little sturdier, but both, to my eye at least, present too rough an appearance for detail. I like them only when I am working on a larger scale.

Drawing pads come in myriad sizes and finishes, of course, and, unusually for me, I find myself choosing the smoother papers, on which the precise drawing of the veins on a leaf or the swelling of a bud, is easier than on rough surfaces.

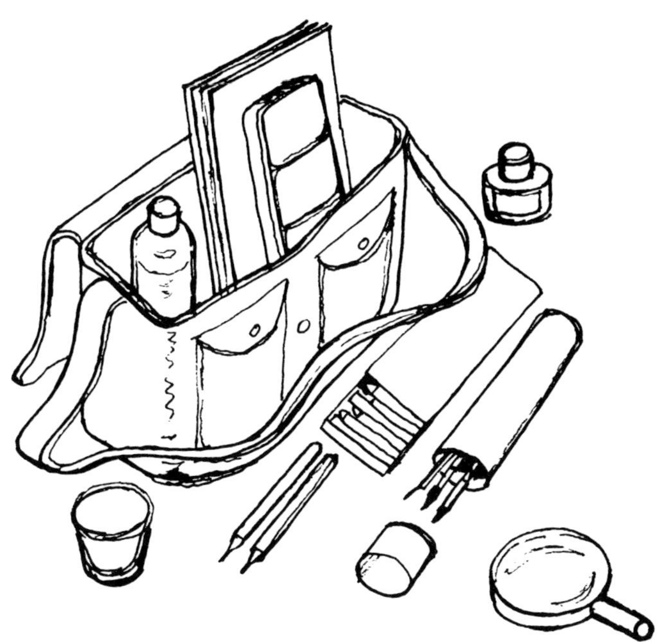

The translucency and freshness of watercolours make them ideal for painting flowers. You can, if you like, carry a large box with dozens of different pans, but you can also achieve a great deal with the sort of miniature box I bought recently in a junk shop. Only a few inches square, with a tiny bottle of water and a slot for a folding brush, it lives in my shirt pocket most of the time, just in case I should happen to see something lovely. A miniature sketch-book as well, and I'm ready to paint the unexpected. Oils are richer in colour – perhaps almost too rich sometimes – and they also require a more elaborate support system in the way of bottles, rags, oil and turpentine and so on.

No matter what the medium, remember always to take along smaller brushes than average. Although you may want to wash in backgrounds with a mop, or paint large flowers with great pigment-laden strokes, you'll rely most of the time, if you're like me, on thin washes and glazes, using round pointed sables, perhaps brush sizes 2 and 4.

I rarely find it necessary to carry an easel. I'm happier with a few drawing pads of different sizes and two or three small canvas boards already primed. But if you are painting large flowering bushes or trees in a garden or a park, try a light packable aluminium one.

Top priority goes to a folding ground sheet. Flower painters spend a good deal of time sitting close to their subjects, which usually means on the ground, or, if you're past the first flush of youth, on a cushion or a low folding stool set on the sheet. And flowers have an exasperating way of growing in bogs or muddy fields, so take your rubber boots too. If you're heading up steep hills or into the mountains, where some of the most beautiful wild flowers grow, you'll need proper climbing shoes and weatherproof gear.

A magnifying glass is also extremely useful for a good clear close-up; to the amateur botanist (which many flower painters become) it's essential for accuracy.

And one last thing: don't forget an identification book, a guide for your area which classifies flowers by easily recognizable visual clues. With the help of a guide and a glass, you soon begin to observe subtleties – an oddly shaped leaf on a tiny stem, the ragged edges of a petal – which sharpen your understanding of the flower as a functional structure as well as a thing of beauty.

Where to go

Finding flowers is not difficult, even in the heart of a city. If you have your own garden you are all set with a year-round supply of subjects, but even without, there is never a shortage. Simply open your eyes.

Look at flower shops, open-air stalls, window boxes, tubs and markets. Although I prefer to paint growing flowers out of doors, there is a great deal to learn – and a lot of pleasure to be had – from painting a bunch of dried flowers or a handsome house plant.

Or think of garden centres. Their owners are usually pleased to welcome an artist. I've often worked for a few days in one, and I say 'thank you' by sketching a plant or a scene in the centre as a little gift for the proprietor.

It can actually be more difficult to find a spot out in the country. Roadside lay-bys may be bordered by lovely wild flowers and escaped garden plants, but they are also noisy and dirty. Farmland is generally privately owned, which means asking permission; few owners will turn down a polite request, unless you want to do something silly, like sitting in the middle of a field of flowering rape on harvest day. Your best bets are the quiet edges of cultivated land,

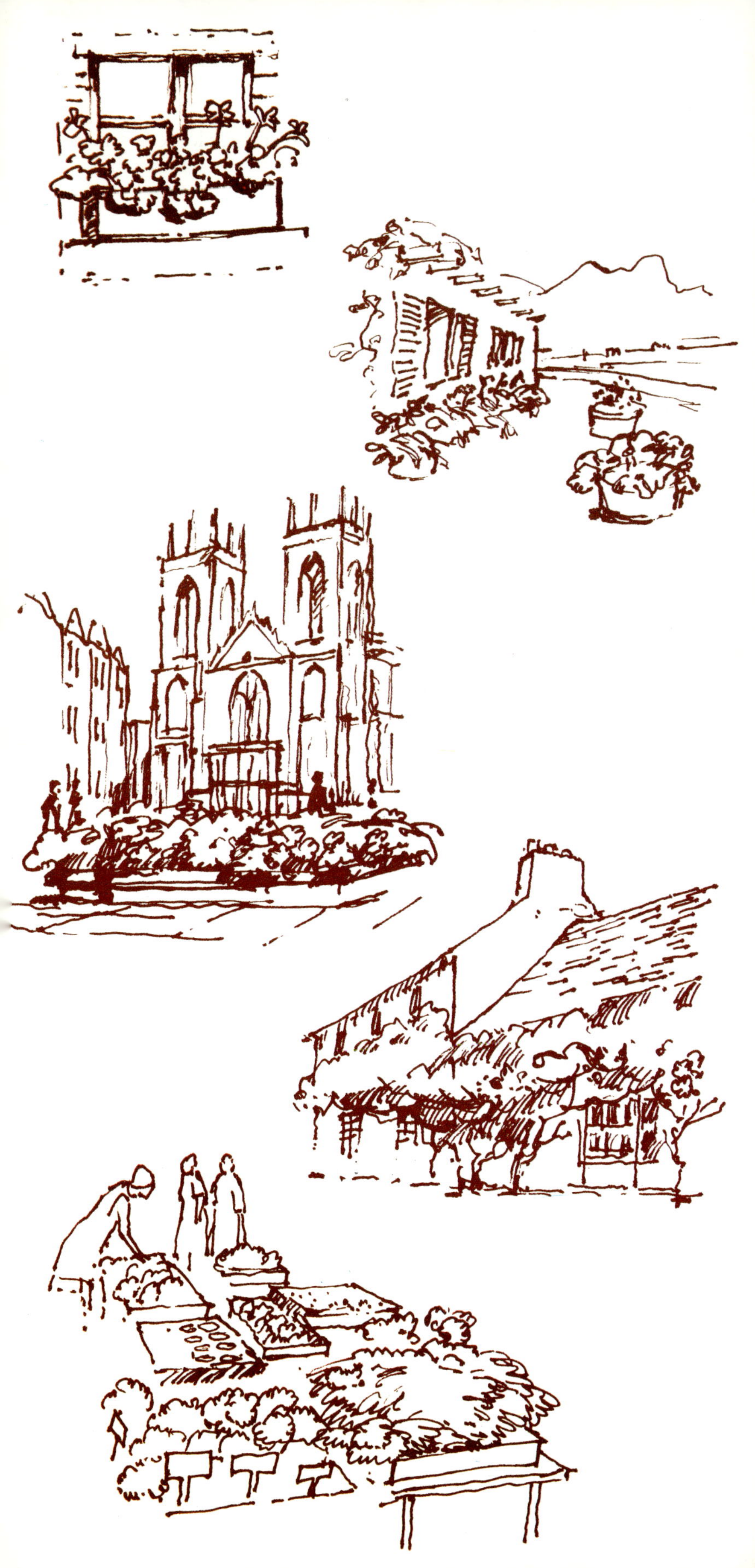

hedgerows and woodlands. And explore a little when you are out on other errands, for exciting places can turn up unexpectedly.

Bear in mind that you are not looking for the grand vista. Flowers, particularly wild flowers, are often small and modestly hidden among tall grasses, in the midst of a tangle of weeds, even in the boggy ground in the bottom of a ditch. But if you are really stumped, without a pink blossom or a purple bract in sight, look closely at the grasses and the trees themselves. All plants have some kind of flower. An ordinary bramble hedge can provide an endless supply of seed pods, berries and blooms.

And don't neglect garden shows, from small local exhibits crammed into a tent, to the vast national shows that could keep you inspired for a year. Take your camera along, to record details that you won't have had time to sketch.

Setting up

Setting up may mean no more than finding a convenient rock, pulling out a pad and a pencil and beginning to draw. But if you are going to spend a few hours, you will need to organize the way you work.

Since you are not looking for the perfect vantage point from which to view a glorious distant horizon, you can concentrate on choosing the most immediately attractive

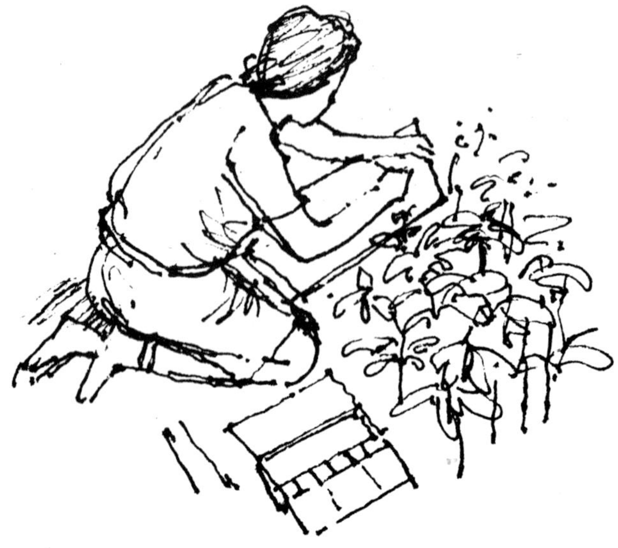

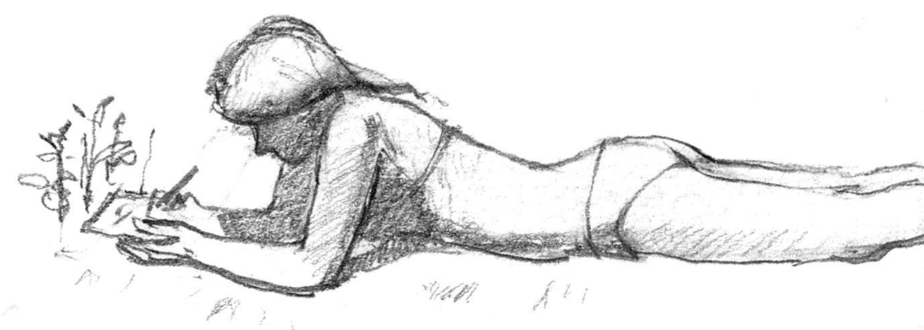

subject. But that may pose problems, too: flowering bushes and trees can blend with each other, and you will need to decide which area to paint.

Then you must arrange your equipment. You want to be near the flowers you have chosen, preferably at a convenient eye level. So spread out your ground sheet, unfold your stool and make a little table of flat stones – I usually pick up a few en route – to keep your paints and pastels off the ground – otherwise they will be at weed and dust height. I've come home all too often to find bits of grass, a dead grasshopper and a drift of pollen in the most inaccessible corners of my box.

Try to work around the flower. You must not twist or turn the stem too much; if you do the flowerhead will be at an unnatural angle, and it will look distorted in the finished painting.

If you can't see the bloom easily, prop an empty canvas or a sheet of paper behind the stem to isolate your subject.

When you are concentrating hard on a small area, you need to stand up and stretch much more often than you do when you work on a large scale and keep moving about. Your fingers can get cramped, too, so take along some hand cream and massage them from time to time to keep the blood circulating.

And if you are out on a beautiful summer's day and become so engrossed with a lovely flower that you forget everything else, try at least to remember that the sun doesn't stop shining to accommodate you. We used to say that you could always tell the still-life painters by their indoor pallor, the landscape painters by their wind-burnt, sun-burnt faces. But you could never miss a flower painter: they were all pale in front and burnt dark on the back.

A wider view

Although choosing a flower calls for a totally different approach to that for choosing a landscape, there are common problems. You don't want to become repetitive in either case. It's boring to paint a single stem or even a spray all the time, so you must strive for variation. Concentrating on the small and precise can become its own trap. You should pull back now and then to take a look at a bank of blossoms or a field of flowering crops before you focus in on one small area.

But working on a small scale also brings rewards. It provides good experience in picking out detail, and it can offer valuable hints about how well a particular medium suits a particular plant.

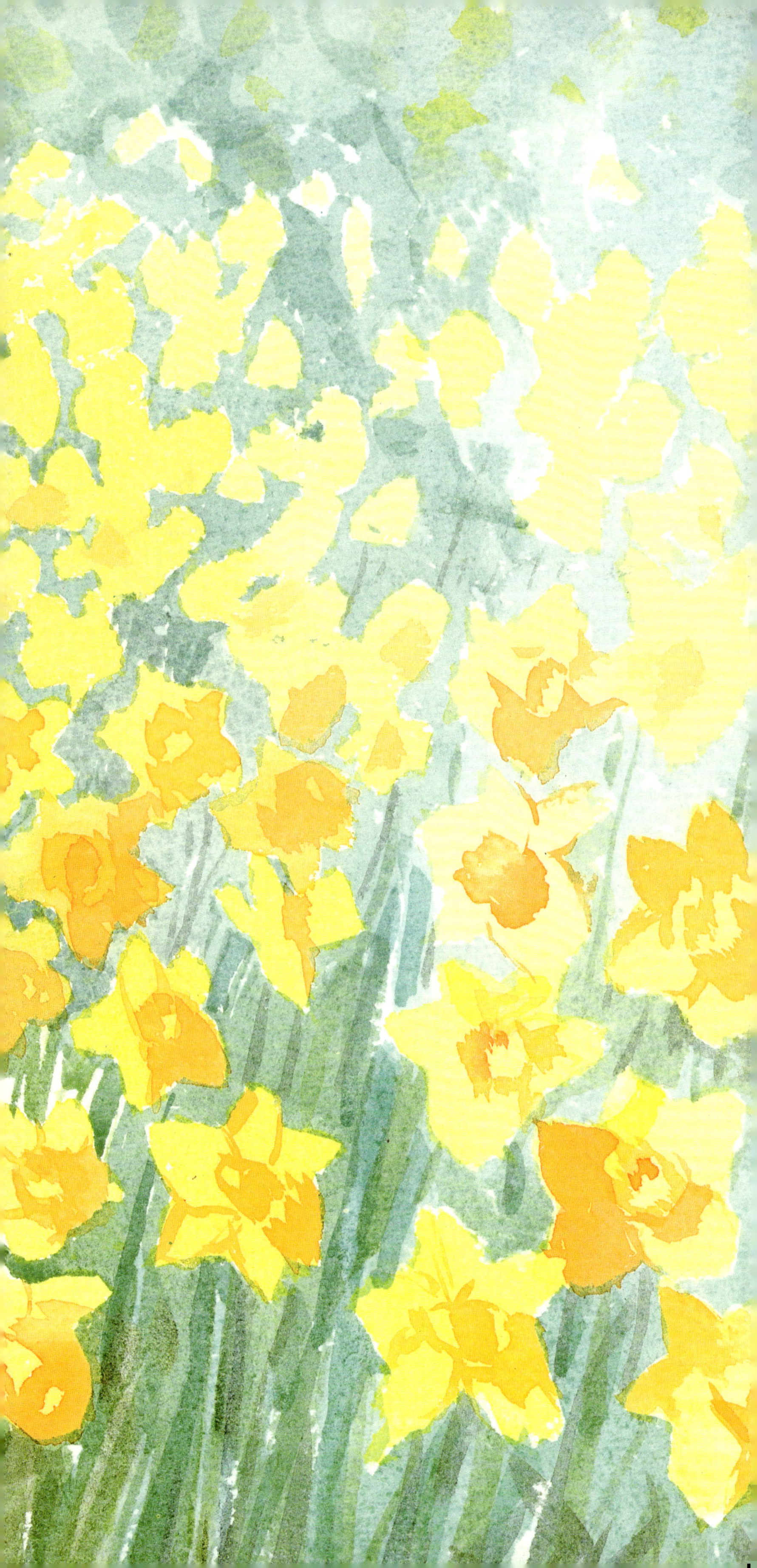

Space and dimension

Although flowers are often stylized as flat patterns, they are obviously part of the round world. But it takes quite a little practice to learn how to re-create the feeling of space and dimension in a drawing that may be no bigger than, say, this page.

Look at your subject carefully. Choose a multi-headed flower like the ragwort below. Each individual flower is a different distance from you, but you haven't the luxury of space that a landscape gives you in which to create a series of receding tones to give the illusion of distance. So you must closely observe the tiny details which convey three dimensions on a two-dimensional surface. Start geographically, with what is farthest from you. That's a good tip for every kind of three-dimensional ink drawing. You can never draw behind things, but you can always superimpose as you move towards the front. Beware of too many crossed stems; this only creates confusion.

Once line drawings seem to work for you, think about other ways of using the three-dimensional space you have established. I spend a good deal of time simply separating out what I want to paint from hazy clouds of leaves and flowers. This isn't as easy as it sounds, because most flowers and bushes grow untidily. There are seldom any strong straight lines to give your picture a natural framework.

Cut around a subject with your eye, choosing the bit you want to take out of the whole – as I did with this bindweed on the opposite page.

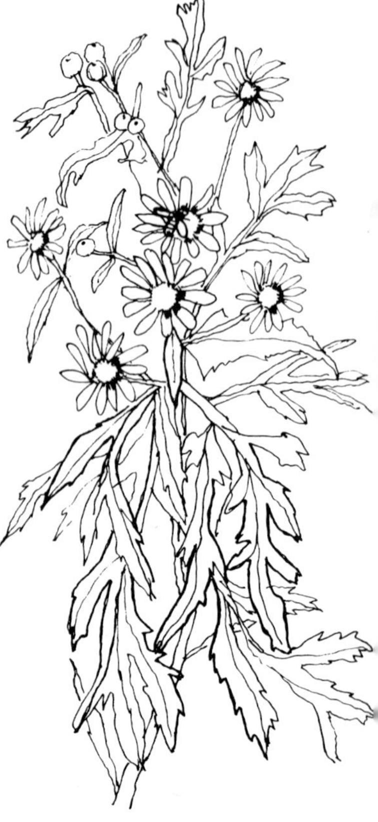

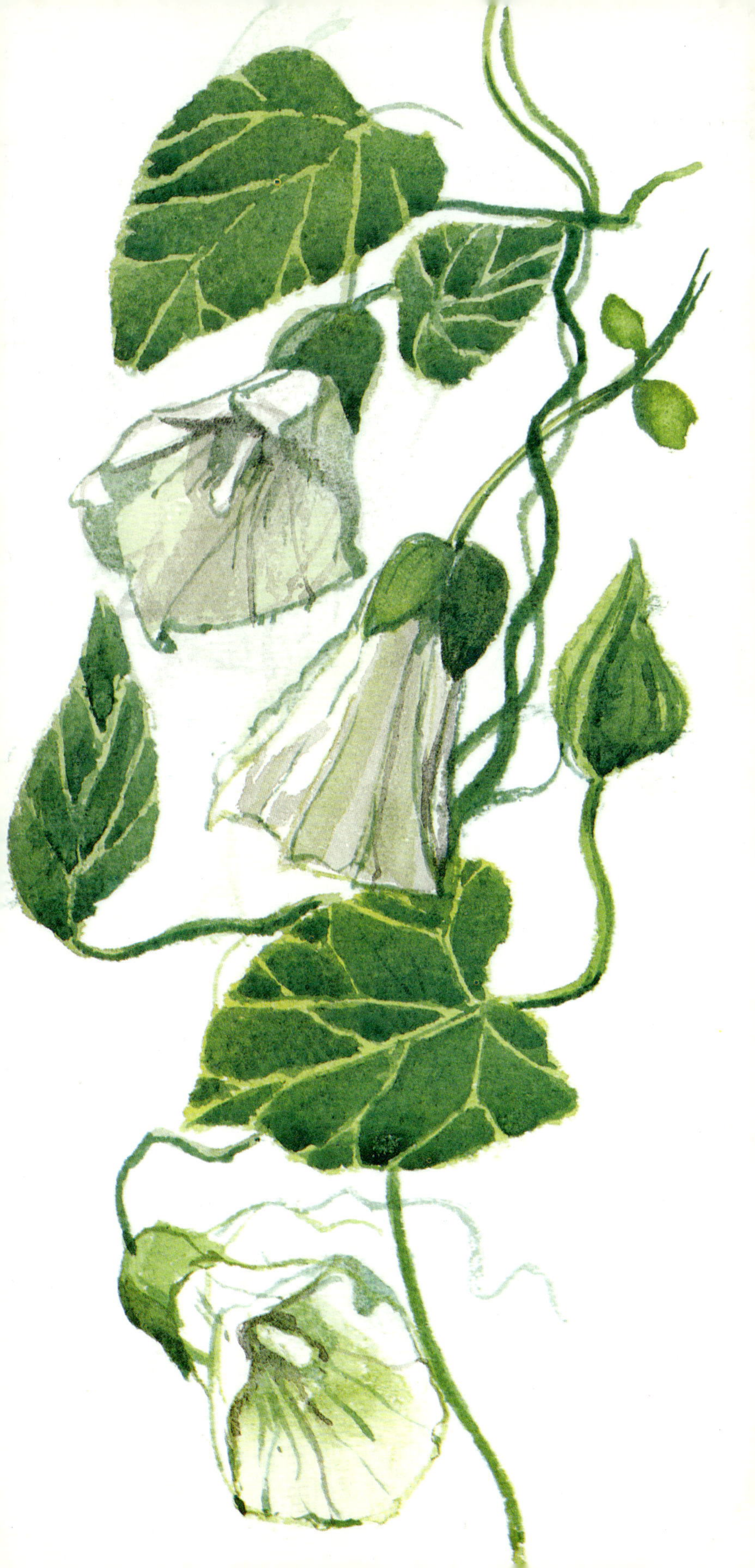

Finding something different

Painting flowers doesn't mean confining yourself to only one style. Keep a fresh and enquiring mind and don't hesitate to change your way of working. If you always do 'portraits' of single flowers, then try big bunches, swathes of meadowland, the huge flowerbeds of a municipal park.

And if you have tried every conceivable way of painting a static picture, why not find out how flowers move?

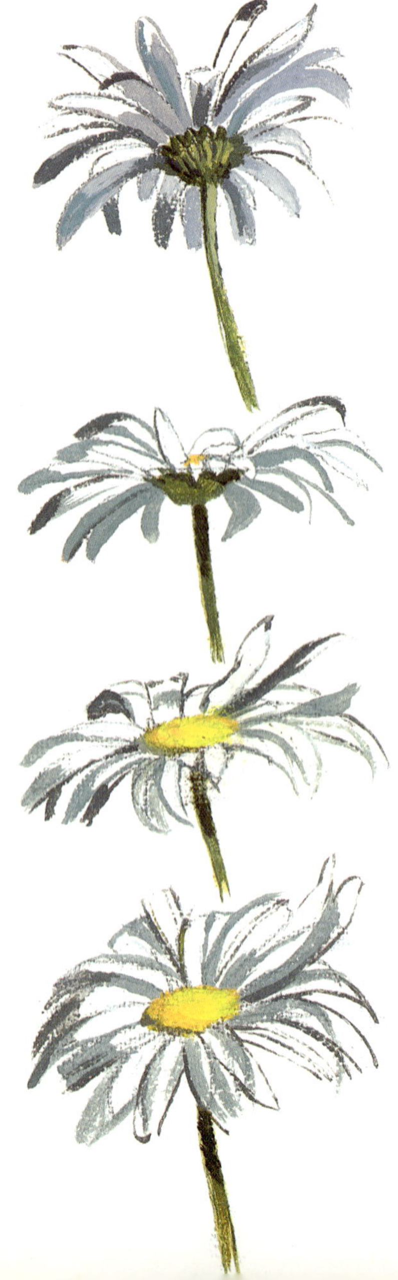

Below are eight studies of the same daisy, turning through the day as the sun passes overhead.

Early one morning, I staked out my position at the end of the lawn. Then all through the day, I went out every hour on the hour to see how the flowerhead had turned. Do the same with any flower that responds to the sun. Or try another experiment: move around the flower yourself, sketching it from eight different viewpoints; then compare those with the eight-hour day of the flower's own movement.

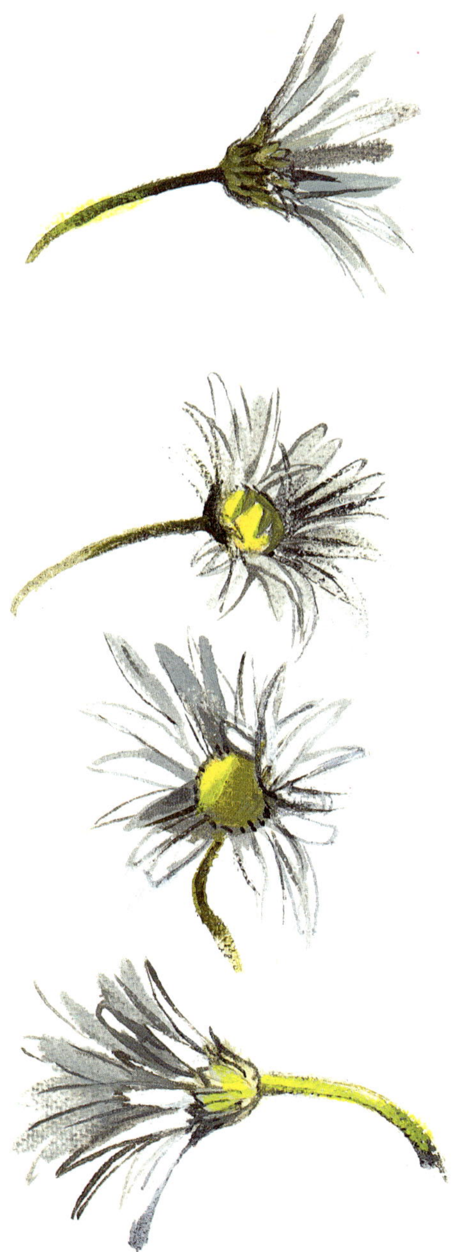

The four seasons colour codes

The colours of nature change with the seasons. We should take advantage of that, painting with the colours appropriate to the time of year – working within the natural palette instead of fighting against it.

I've used the single branch of an apple tree to indicate briefly what happens throughout the year: the first buds of spring; the flowers of early summer; the fruit of the autumn and the bare stems of winter.

Of course, the medium you use will affect the quality of the colour and the texture of the finished painting. I prefer working with watercolours in the spring and winter, and with oils during the summer and autumn. This has, I think, to do with the texture of the pigment. The light fresh look of watercolour can convey brightness in the spring and cold in the winter, but it seldom produces the heavy richness of tone that we see all around us during the summer and autumn.

The codes show how colours can be mixed and matched to create the effects you want. If you hold them next to flowers in bloom during the appropriate season, there should be a natural blending of tone and intensity. While it is perfectly possible to paint in summer colours whilst looking at a winter tree, I think you would find the results curiously unsatisfactory.

Remember that the codes are a guideline for your eye as you begin to paint outdoors, and there will always be exceptions. An early rose in May can be as deep a gold as any autumn chrysanthemum, and you will surely find a few, pale, delicate pink blackberry blossoms alongside the rich purple autumn berries we show.

But as you learn what to expect on your flower-hunting trips, so your own personal palette will develop, based on the climate and natural growth pattern of the plants you find.

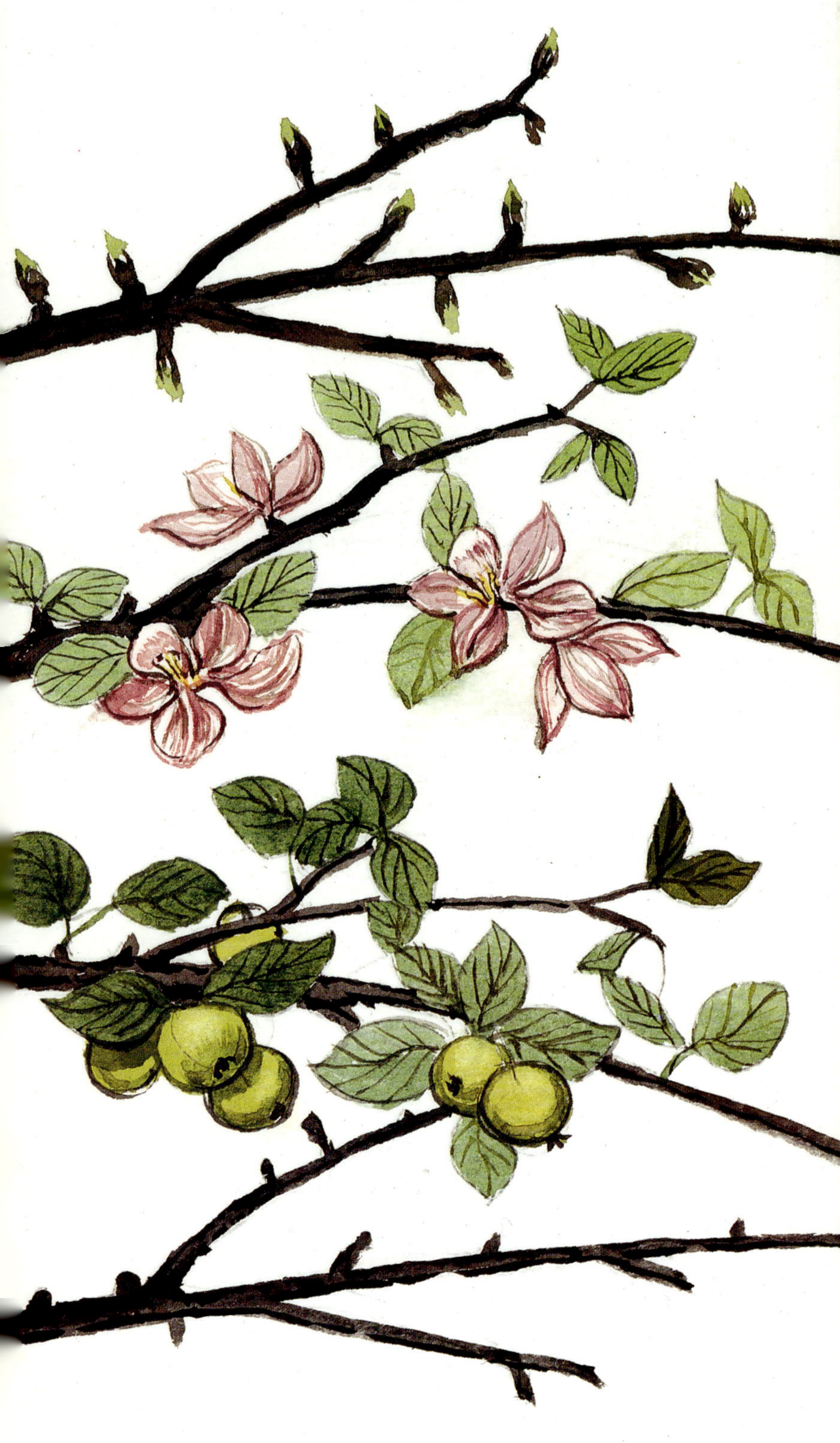

The spring palette

Spring is the time of new leaves, young buds, tightly furled leaves and the heady feeling of growth and promise. All perhaps slightly romantic, but nature has a way of fulfilling our most basic clichés. So you will need fresh colours – greens, yellows and the pinky purples that you find in wild flowers and clovers.

Work carefully when you make up your spring palette. It's a deceptive time of year. I have often put down the first leaves too quickly and found that I had the right colour but the wrong tone. Flowers are still new and the ground is not really warm enough to provide much heat, so everything is clearer and more transparent than it is in summer.

The light is difficult too, changing quickly according to the weather. Mist, especially in the mornings, can be a nuisance. Damp weather affects your paper as well as your feet. Watercolours will spread and become difficult to control. But this has its compensations; it creates a kind of impressionism that adapts well to spring conditions: pale sunlight on new greens; white flowers looking almost ghostly pale; pearly mist, and a feeling that if you held your breath the world would stop. Well, slow down, anyway.

Using light washes of primary colours will keep your tones from being muddy. Chinese white on watercolour may be too heavy; try letting the paper stay white for the best results. This is not the time of year for tinted papers; stick to pure white for the freshest effect.

I find the mornings and evenings best for springtime painting, with the chance to see the flowers opening in the first light and glistening with dew. The weather also seems more predictable – fairly quiet, even when the night has been a deluge of rain and the day blustery.

But do protect yourself. The ground still holds winter damp, and dewdrops on your paper can menace fine details.

The following colour code uses light washes of watercolour, above, and scraped-down pastels, below.

Viridian green 3 Prussian blue 1	Viridian green 3 Lemon yellow 1	Alizarin crimson	Indian red 2 Burnt sienna 2	Cadmium yellow
Raw umber	Yellow ochre	Cobalt blue	Indian red 3 Cerulean blue 1	Ultramarine blue
Raw sienna	Cerulean blue	Cadmium orange 3 Cerulean blue 1	Viridian green	Viridian green 3 Yellow ochre 1
Prussian blue	Lemon yellow	Raw sienna 3 Cadmium orange 1	Yellow ochre 3 Raw umber 1	Viridian green 3 Cerulean blue 1
Cerulean blue	Orange	Light pink	Deep grey	Bright yellow
Deep ochre	Bright green	Light ochre	Light blue	Yellow ochre
Deep pink	Cadmium yellow 2 Light pink 2	Sap green	Light green	Viridian green
Purple	Sea green	Cobalt blue, light	Deep blue	Peach

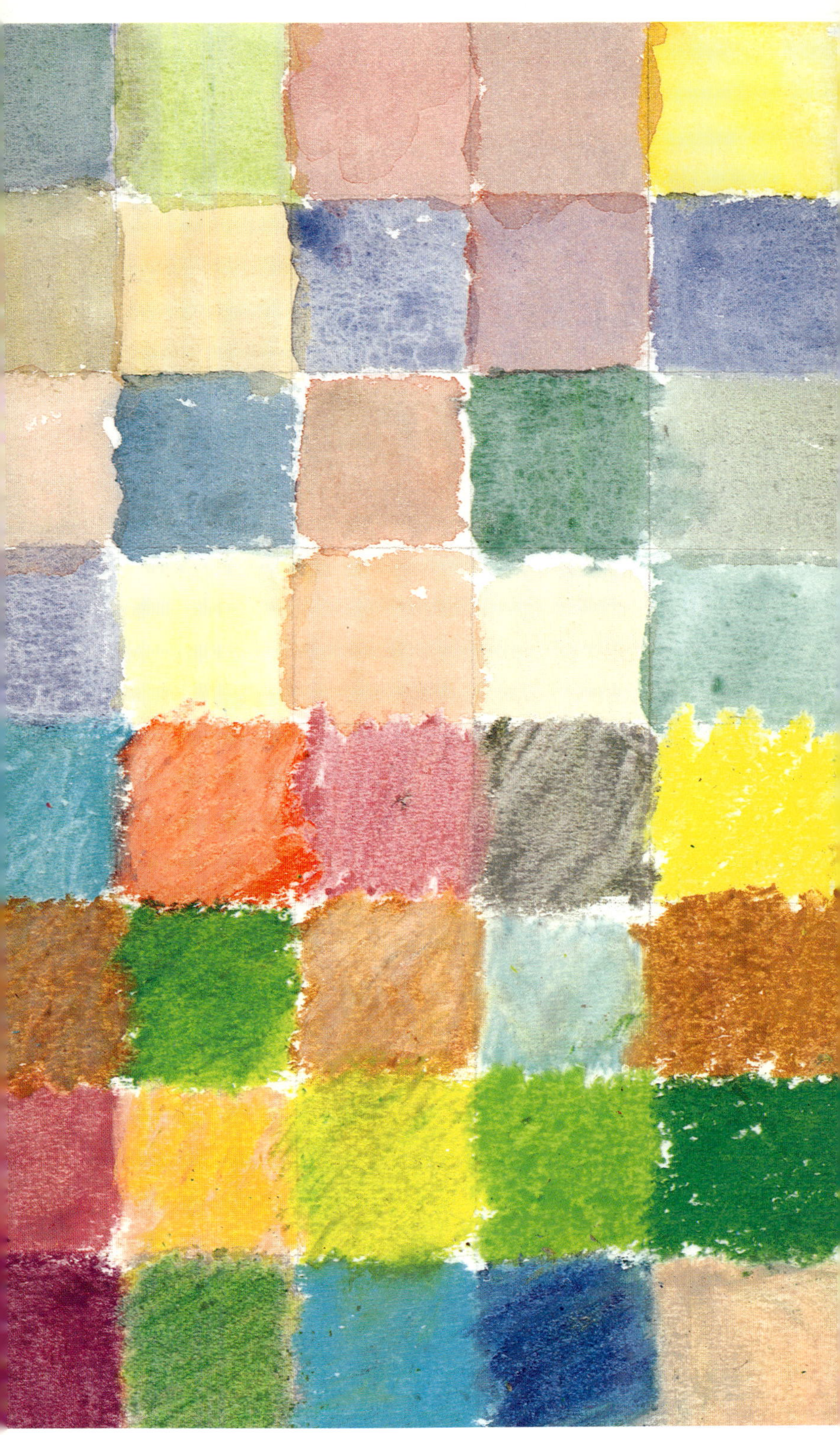

The summer palette

Summer means a brush loaded with bright, deep, rich colours. Almost everything that blooms, bursts out with an abandon never seen in the spring. The artist, whether in town or village, sees flowers everywhere – in the profusion of an old-fashioned garden or the formal beds of a public park.

This is a good time to dry everlasting flowers from your own garden. Many keep their rich reds and yellows even after they have been dried. Heliotropes are much in demand for flower arrangements, but I like to see them lying naturally in a heap, as if they had just been pulled out of the ground.

It's a curious fact that during the height of summer it can be difficult to track down wild flowers. Part of the explanation is surely natural – most flowers bloom in the spring, are pollinated and fruit or go to seed in the summer, and store up food through their leaves for the winter to come. However, human beings must also take part of the blame, as heavy commercial spraying of cropping plants kills many summer flowers which are regarded as weeds.

So do cultivate your garden, and your neighbour's garden as well. Plant window boxes with geraniums if you live in the city, or buy inexpensive annuals to grow quickly in tubs.

Summer is also wonderful at any seaside town – for the glorious changes of light, of course, but also because many seaside towns have charming botanical gardens, imaginative beds and tubs and even the sometimes derided (but to me, delightful) botanical clocks or town names spelled out in flowers. They often hold flower festivals, and holiday visitors can make a record with sketch-book and camera of unusual flowers that are not native to their own towns.

If you can't get away, summer is a good time to pay another visit to your local garden centre; the annuals that weren't sold at the beginning of the season are usually in full bloom, and the shrubs in their containers are burgeoning.

The following colour code uses heavy pastels, above, and oil paints, sometimes scraped down, below.

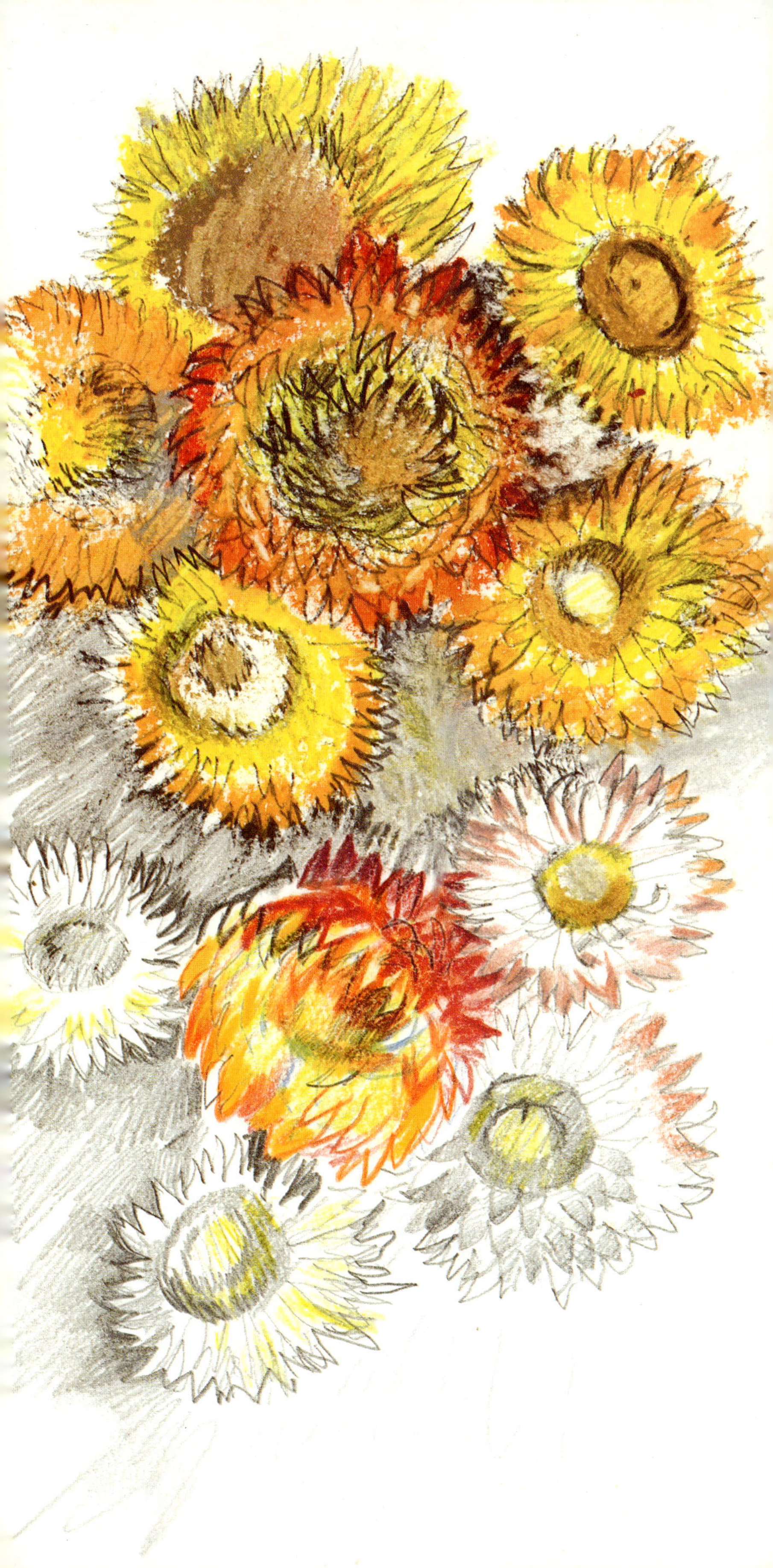

Cadmium orange	Cadmium red 1 White 3	Cadmium red	Yellow ochre, deep	Plum purple
Olive green 3 Light ochre 1	Cadmium orange 3 Raw sienna 1	Cadmium red 1 Yellow ochre 3	Light red	Cerulean blue
Plum purple 3 Burnt umber 1	Deep purple	Cadmium orange	Prussian blue 1 White 3	Viridian green 1 Yellow ochre 2
Viridian green	Cadmium yellow, deep	Cadmium yellow	Cobalt blue	Orange 3 Light grey 1
Cobalt blue 1 White 3	Hooker's green 3 White 1	Alizarin crimson 2 Raw sienna 2	Cadmium orange	Viridian green 3 Raw umber 1
Yellow ochre 2 Cadmium orange 2	Cadmium red	Cadmium orange 3 Raw sienna 1	Yellow ochre 3 Burnt sienna 1	Raw sienna
Viridian green 3 Cobalt blue 1	Ultramarine blue	Alizarin crimson 3 Raw sienna 1	Alizarin crimson	Cobalt blue 2 Zinc white 2
Indian red 3 Raw sienna 2	Viridian green	Hooker's green	Cobalt blue	Cadmium yellow, deep

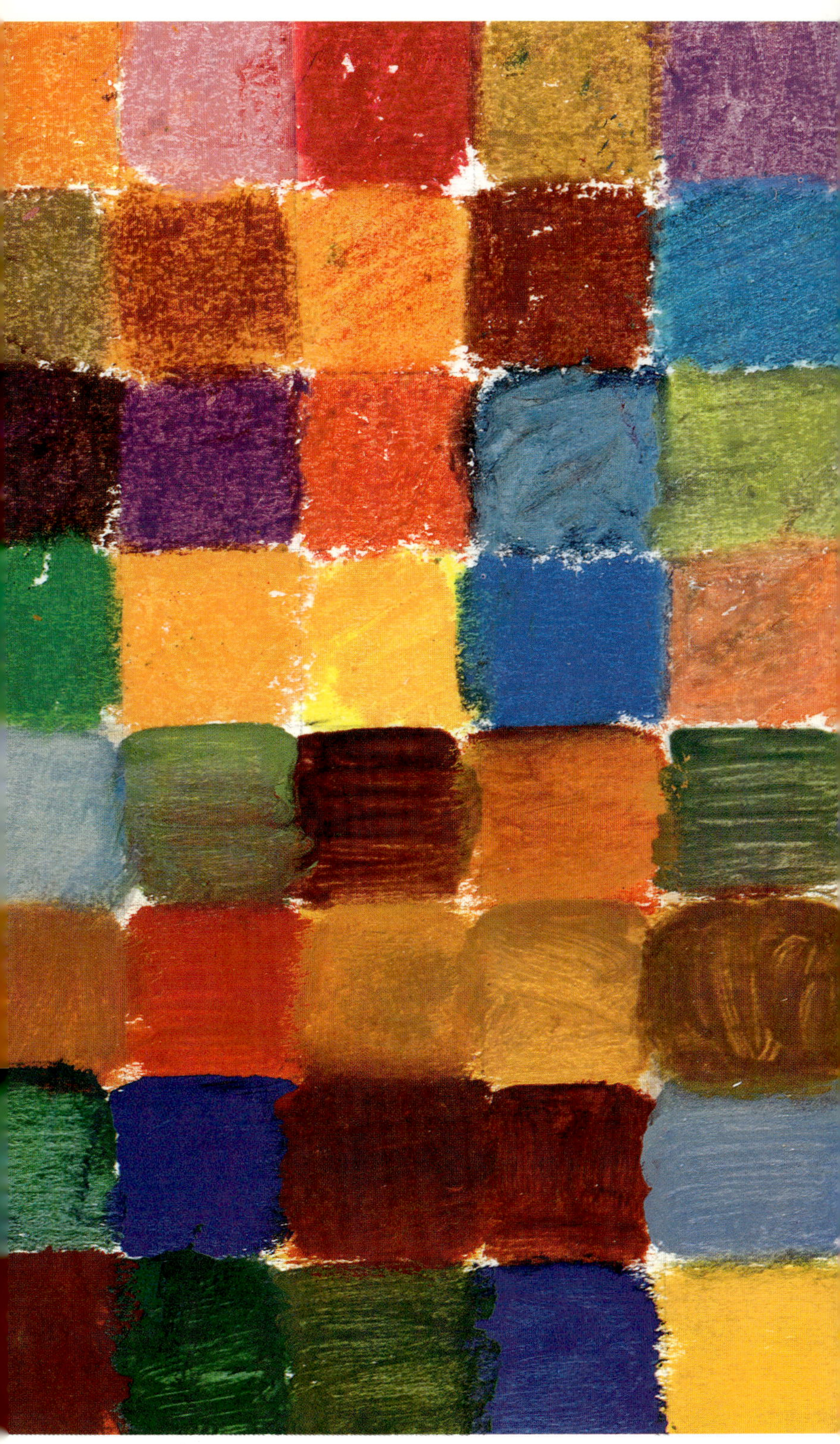

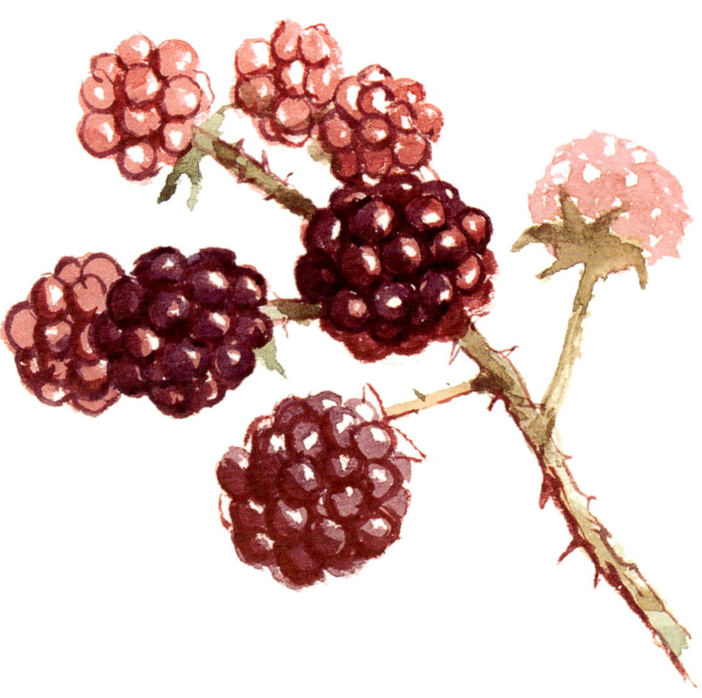

The autumn palette

Fiery colours and deep rich tones herald the autumn season. Nature displays them everywhere, as plants are harvested and the trees whose leaves turn colour before dying become flaming torches. Autumn flowers grow in the same colours, although the development of greater variety in our garden plants has also given us spring-pink dahlias and chrysanthemums.

Out in the fields, however, it becomes a little difficult to find flowers, and you must search for places where summer lingers. Blackberries are one of my favourite subjects, and you often find late flowers and ripe berries growing together on the same thorny branch. Roses have turned into hips – like the berries, fruit rather than flowers. But they reveal one more stage in the life of the plant, so why not paint them, too?

I use oils almost exclusively when I paint out of doors in the autumn. However, I make the effort to do a few watercolours or pastels every month, and I am always surprised at just how rich and ripe both mediums can be.

The following colour code uses watercolour, above, and layered oil paints, below.

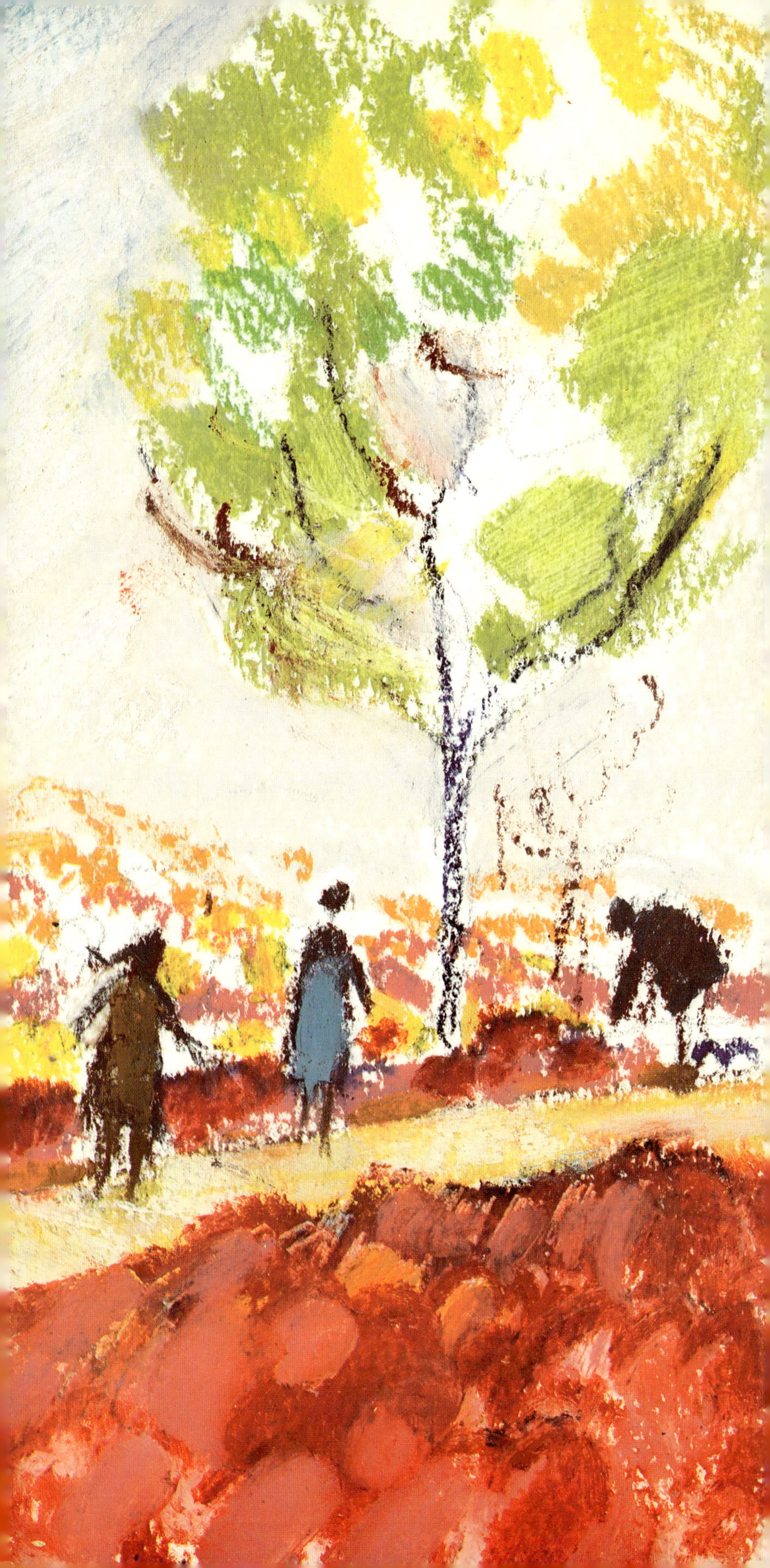

Cadmium red	Burnt sienna	Cadmium orange	Burnt umber	Viridian green
Deep purple	Cadmium orange, deep	Cobalt blue 3 Prussian blue 1	Viridian green 3 Cerulean blue 1	Raw sienna
Viridian green 1 Yellow ochre 3	Purple	Olive green 3 Raw sienna 1	Cobalt blue	Raw sienna 3 Viridian green 1
Yellow ochre	Burnt sienna	Cobalt blue 3 Ivory black 1	Yellow ochre 3 Raw sienna 1	Alizarin crimson 1 Raw sienna 3
Orange 3 Deep ochre 1	Deep red 2 Black 2	Bright red 3 Black 1	Bright yellow 3 Orange 1	Deep ochre
Deep blue	Deep blue 1 Orange 3	Deep blue 3 Indian red 1	Bright green	Purple
Bright red 3 Bright green 1	Deep blue 2 Purple 2	Yellow ochre	Deep blue 1 Black 3	Deep orange
Scarlet	Aqua 1 Indian red 3	Deep green	Deep blue 2 Black 2	Bright red

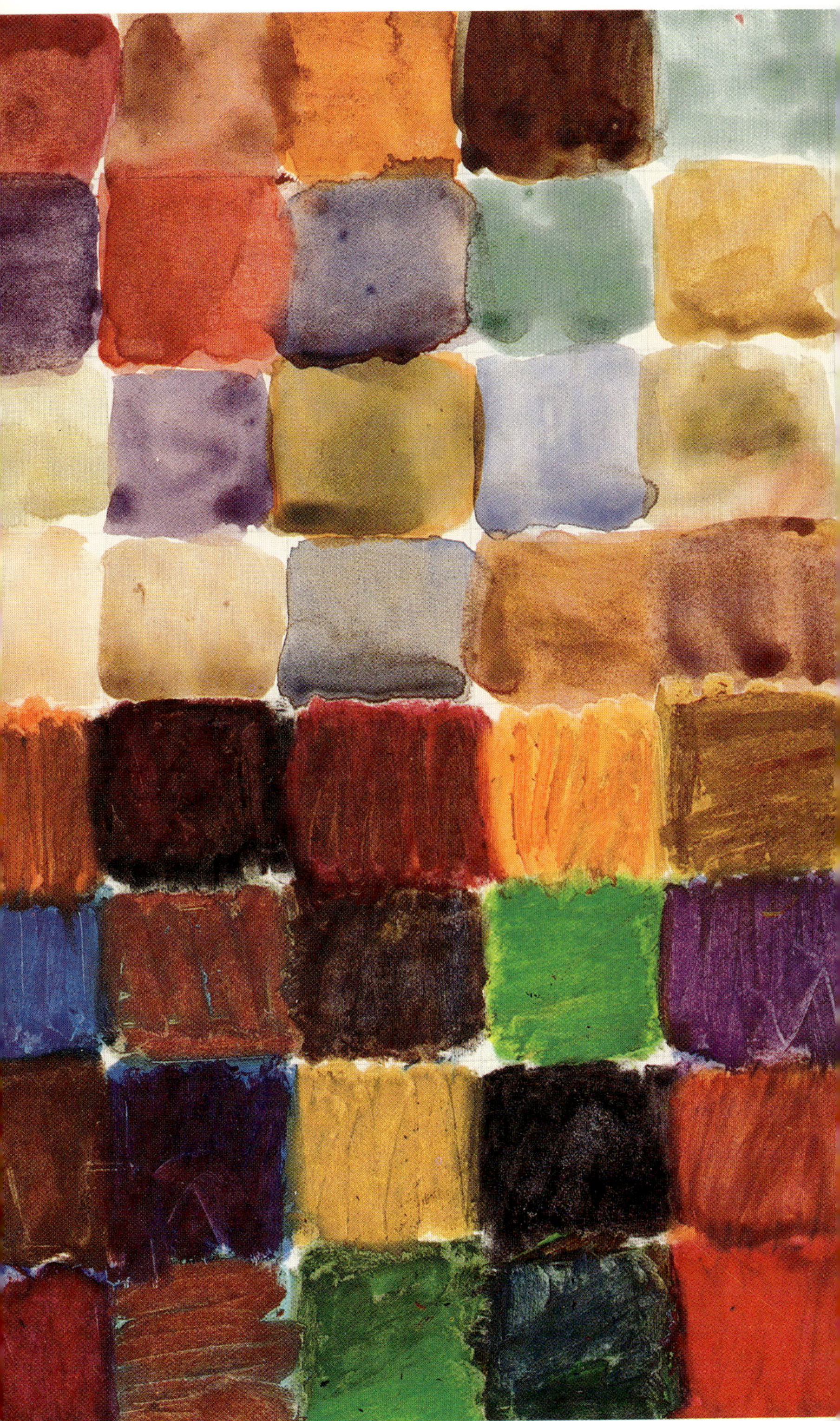

The winter palette

Cold dark earth, dark skies, dead branches – we tend to think of winter as a time of no colour at all, a monochrome in blacks, whites and greys. But this is far from true; everywhere you look (well perhaps not in the Arctic Circle) there are delicate and subtle colours: blues, reds, and olive greens, even pinks, and many varieties of brown and sienna.

The brown of this large weed was particularly rich and satisfying in colour, and I found it easy to do with a single felt-tip pen. There are many different shades of brown and black; using only one can make a dramatic picture.

Winter flowers are hard to find if you are counting on blossoms and green leaves. Those that brave the winds and storms are small and inconspicuous, easy to miss when you are freezing and so bundled up that you can barely get your fingers around the carrying handle of your paintbox, let alone around a brush. But persevere – the colour range is remarkable once you stand still long enough to notice.

There are compensations, even for the less hardy, for forcing yourself out into the crisp cold air. Chilly weather, so long as it isn't raining, is perfect for deft watercolour strokes that capture the feeling of ice and frost. The paper never gets soggy, the paintings dry quickly, and, if you are impatient enough to stack them before they are dry, the paint will freeze into a thin film on the surface, and the sheets can be gently prised apart without damage.

Nonetheless, you should be prepared for some discomfort. When you are struggling across a muddy ice-covered field, looking for that one, small flower in the midst of a far-off hedge, you may envy the landscape artist, sketching a vista from the warm seat of a car or a protected porch.

But if even a cheerful, snowy, sunny winter's day is too cold to tempt you out, think about painting dried flowers. This sprig had dried out naturally on its stem in my garden, but you can now get dried flowers all year long in florist shops, garden centres, gift shops and even supermarkets.

The following colour code uses watercolour, above, and layered oil paints, below.

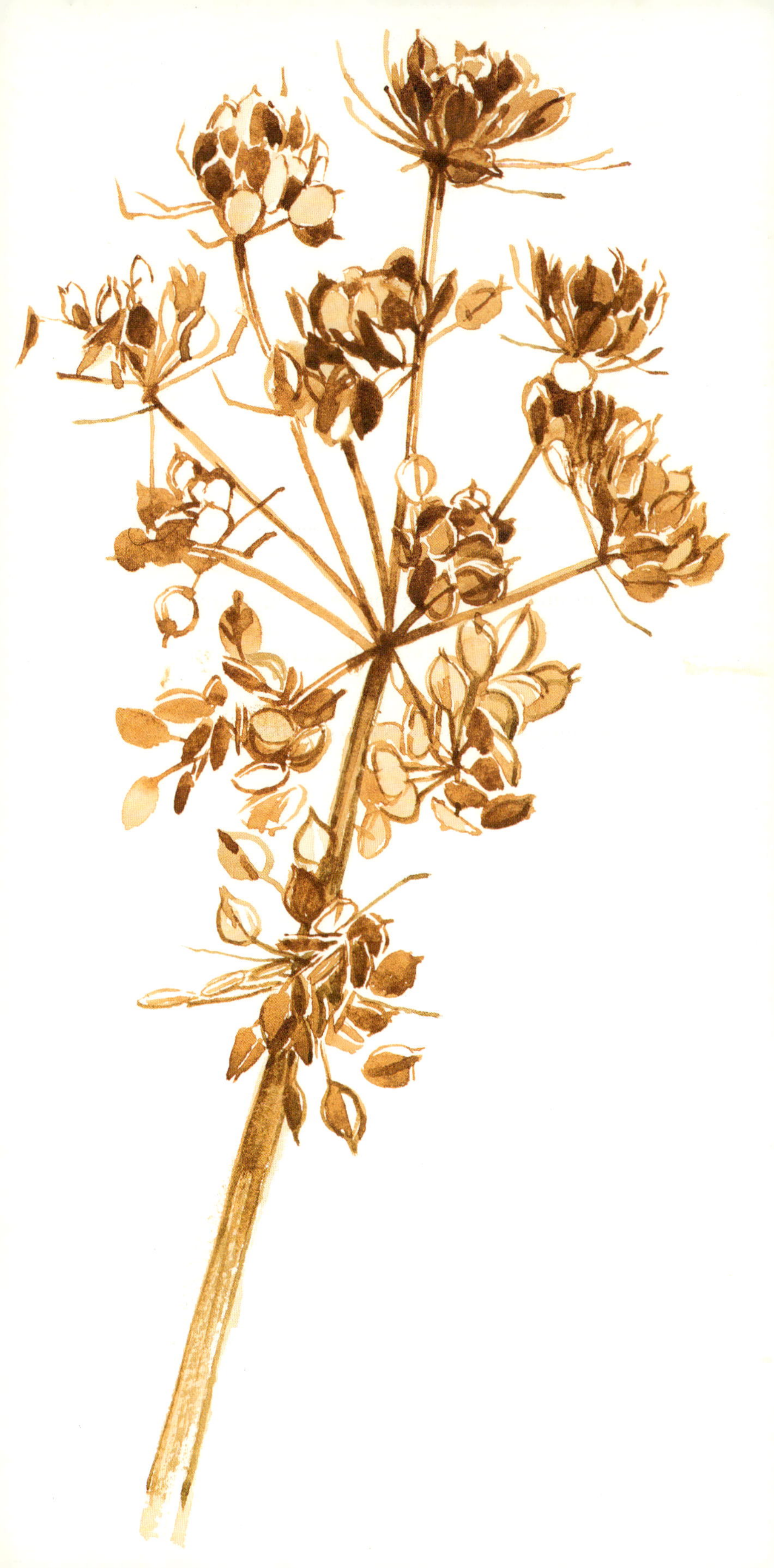

Indian red 3 Ivory black 1	Lemon yellow 3 Ivory black 1	Raw umber 3 Ivory black 1	Raw umber 1 Ivory black 3	Ivory black Water
Raw umber 2 Ivory black 2	Cobalt blue 2 Ivory black 2	Indian red 2 Burnt umber 2	Yellow ochre 3 Raw umber 1	Raw sienna 3 Ivory black 1
Ultramarine blue 3 Ivory black 1	Yellow ochre 3 Raw umber 1	Ultramarine blue 2 Ivory black 2	Viridian green 3 Ivory black 1	Cobalt blue 1 Ivory black 3
Alizarin crimson 3 Burnt umber 1	Cadmium red 3 Raw umber 1	Ultramarine blue 3 Raw umber 1	Raw sienna 3 Burnt umber 1	Viridian green 3 Raw sienna 1
Alizarin crimson 3 Lamp black 1	Lamp black 1 Titanium white 3	Alizarin crimson 1 Titanium white 3	Ivory black 1 Zinc white 3	Lamp black 1 Indian red 1 Zinc white 2
Cobalt blue 3 Ivory black 1	Light red 2 Zinc white 2	Prussian blue 3 Lamp black 1	Lamp black 1 Zinc white 3	Indian red 1 Zinc white 3
Ivory black 2 Raw umber 1 Zinc white 1	Lamp black 2 Viridian 1 Zinc white 1	Venetian red 2 Raw umber 2	Cobalt blue 1 Ivory black 1 Titanium white 2	Ivory black 1 Raw umber 1 Cobalt blue 1 Zinc white 1
Hooker's green 3 Ivory black 1	Venetian red 2 Zinc white 2	Lemon yellow 3 Lamp black 1	Prussian blue 1 Ivory black 2 Zinc white 1	Cobalt blue 2 Zinc white 1

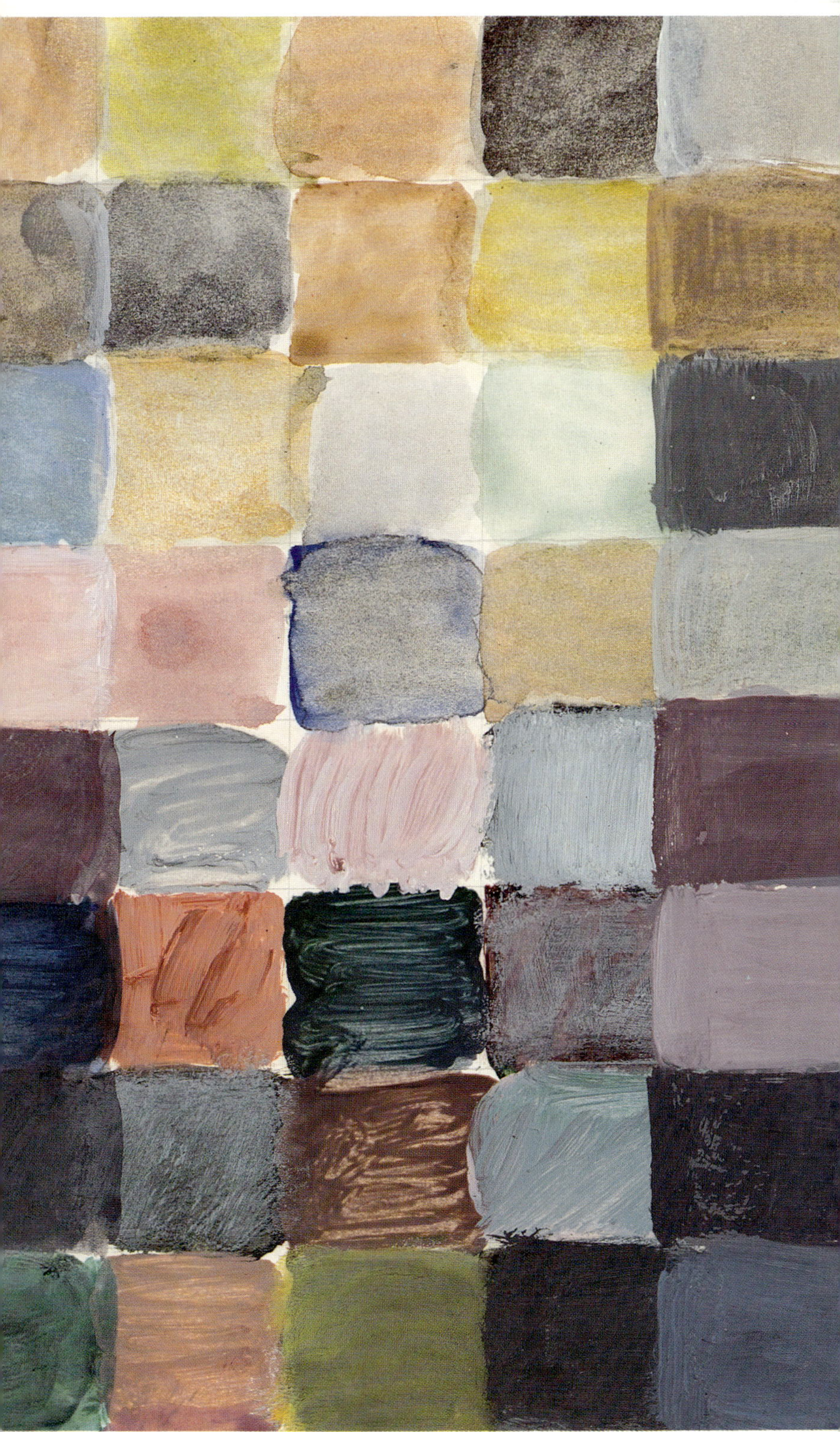

Techniques

Sketching quickly

When you work out of doors, conditions are likely to change very quickly, and you must be able to switch from thinking about a major project to recognizing by the black thunderclouds in the sky that you might have only five minutes before you are drenched. That is not much, but it can be quite long enough at least to make a sketch of impressions you want to take away with you.

Sketching in a hurry presents two problems – choice of medium and of technique. Pencils, pens or pastels might seem the obvious tools because they come out of their boxes all ready to use. That holds true for pencils and for felt-tipped pens, a sensible alternative to coloured inks and drawing pens.

But beware of pastels. For one thing, they smudge easily. Working quickly, you might become careless, brushing the paper with your hand or your sleeve and blurring your lines. Quite pleasant as an effect – but not necessarily the effect you want. Another problem: pastels must be fixed, which isn't practical if you are in a tearing hurry.

Surprisingly, oils can work wonders at speed. All it takes is a quick-drying gel mixed into the pigment – not too much pigment and a little extra turpentine to thin the paint down. Oil sketches can be done on canvas or on specially prepared paper pads, and paper palettes can be used once and then folded to keep the left-over paint from staining your clothes.

This little oil sketch was done in exactly four minutes. It shows how much atmosphere you can capture with none of the details on which we have concentrated throughout most of this book. The overwhelming impression is what counts – an abundance of brilliant colour, vitality, growth and sunlight, even though there is no sun in the painting, and scarcely more than a glimpse of sky. With oil or acrylic paints, work the dark background on to the canvas in quick brush-strokes, splash in the flowerheads, and only then mark out the lighter highlights of the stems and leaves. Give yourself a time limit – ten minutes at the most – and stop when it is up, no matter how little you have done.

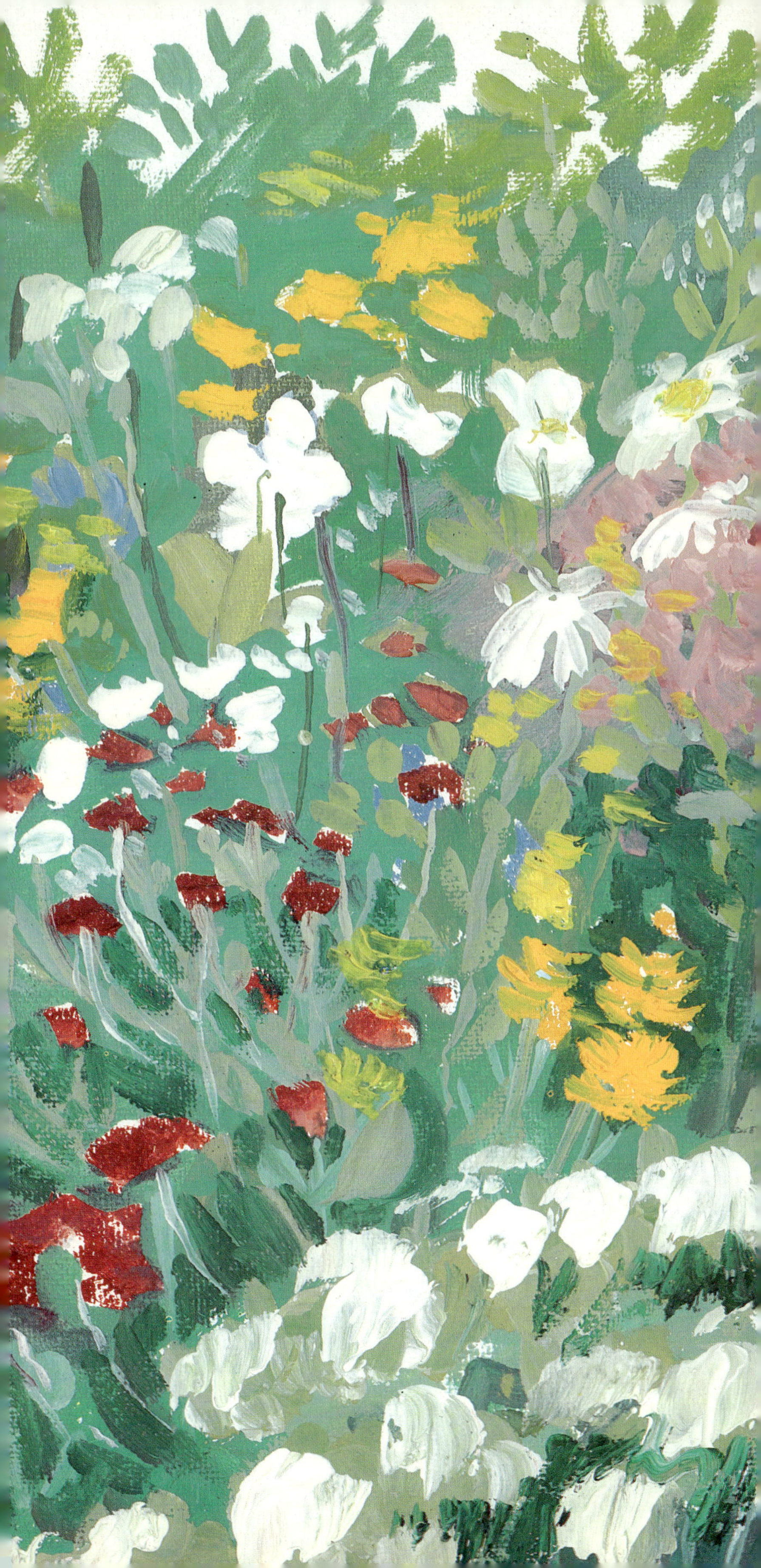

Working slowly

Given reasonable weather and enough time and space to set out your equipment, making careful studies of flowers can be marvellously rewarding. Working in detail helps you to understand how flowers are structured, how they are alike and how they differ from each other, and what problems you are likely to encounter.

Take sweet peas, for instance. They are lovely in the garden, both for scent and colour. Unhappily, I have no recipe for capturing their scent in a picture, but with colour we are dealing with something truly amenable to the painter's art.

The sweet peas in the picture were a deep variety of purple and red, and I painted their petals in quite heavy watercolour. I would ordinarily have used much more water to give a transparent appearance, but this spray was so vivid that I could see it distinctly from the far end of the garden, and I wanted to convey that intensity.

For the same reason, I kept the background white, even though I painted the flowers out of doors against a dark evergreen hedge. You can try backgrounds of different colours, but to get the strongest effect white is unbeatable.

It's a small painting, but it took quite a long time – over two hours. I used the lightest of pencil marks, merely to indicate the spatial dimensions. Outlines, even in faint pencil, would have been disconcertingly visible in the finished work.

The pigment was laid down in a series of almost dry layers, straight from the tube with a very fine brush. It is a technique more often used with thin oil than with the broader washes of watercolour; you must load your brush fairly carefully before every stroke, and it takes some practice to perfect.

Try working on a single bud first. Even though the paint is dry, you must wait patiently before you can add the shadows of the crinkled petal.

Even this technique is not as precise as the kind of realistic painting that reproduces the flower exactly as you see it. To try achieving that, you will probably have to take the flower back to the studio. There is too much movement and too many changes of light in the garden, no matter how still and bright the day.

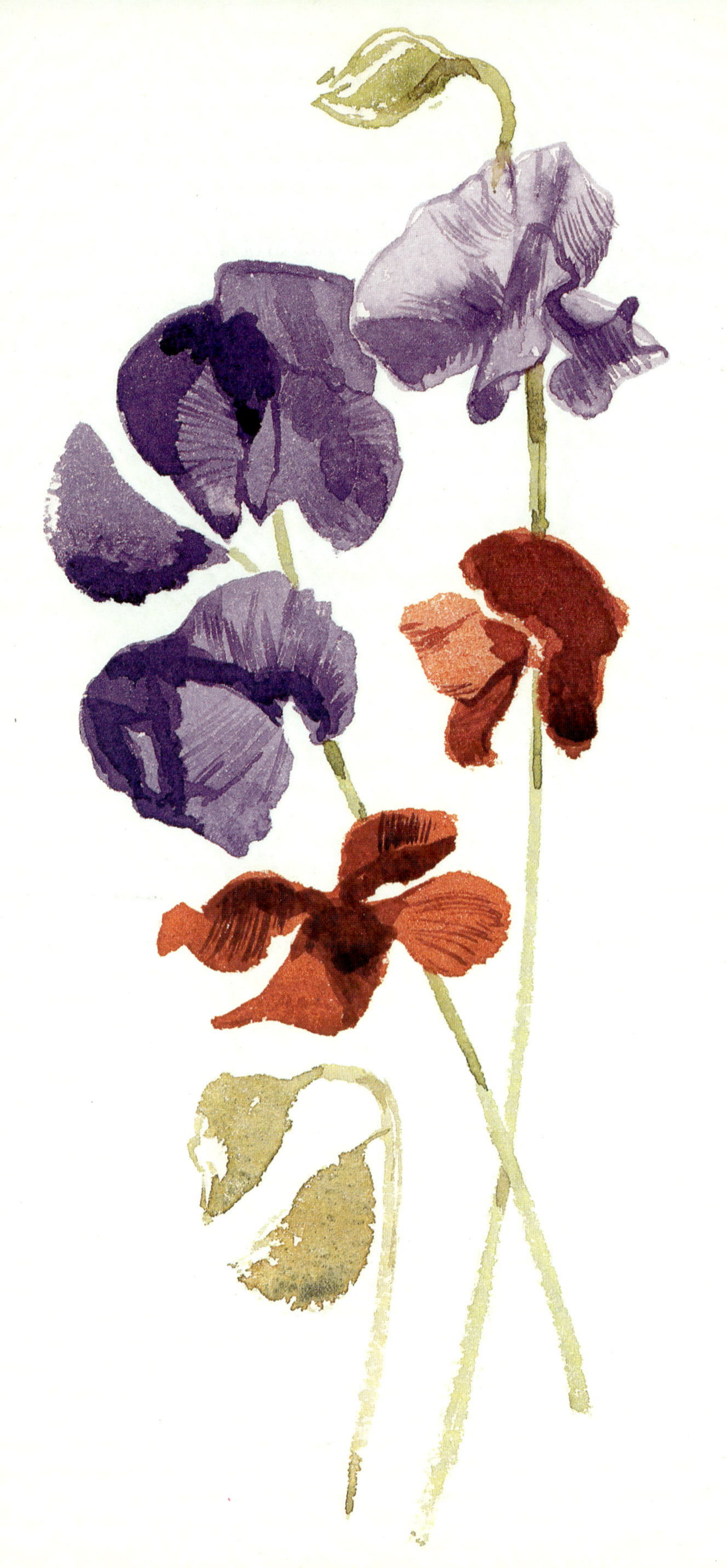

Precise observation

Unless you are reasonably experienced, don't try to work with one single leaf at a time. Our eyes are not accustomed to seeing precisely without some sort of reference. Observing the differences of texture, shape, the edges and vein structures in three or four varieties of leaf makes it easier to see how each of the plants on which they grow has its own design.

Put down all the basic shapes first, and then draw each leaf separately. You are making a comparative study rather than one picture of several leaves. Your eyes should travel constantly from one to the other as you draw, checking that you understand the variations of each feature.

You may find it useful to consult a botanical book, but try not to do any serious study before you paint. Certainly, you should take a book on your trips to find wild flowers, just to make sure you don't dig up or destroy any rare or scarce species – but if you study a picture or a painting before starting to work, you will without realizing it, be influenced by what was on the page, and your eye will take a rest.

That is the last thing you want to happen. On the contrary, you need to sharpen every perception so that the tiniest change in each leaf tip, the detail of an insect egg or the curling shape of a spore will become as familiar as the blowsy shape of a giant sunflower or an open rose.

Learn to look for details which are representative of a particular plant; tiny hairs on the surface give grey plants their characteristic woolly effect; the glossy sheen on an evergreen intensifies the colour and creates a kind of waxy surface which can be translated into light patches on a drawing or painting.

Making comparative studies of this sort can be excellent training for the eye. Once you can work happily with the leaves of three or four different plants, try three or four leaves of the same plant. This is more subtle. There will be a general likeness, but there are minute differences in the way each leaf grows that will make it an exciting project.

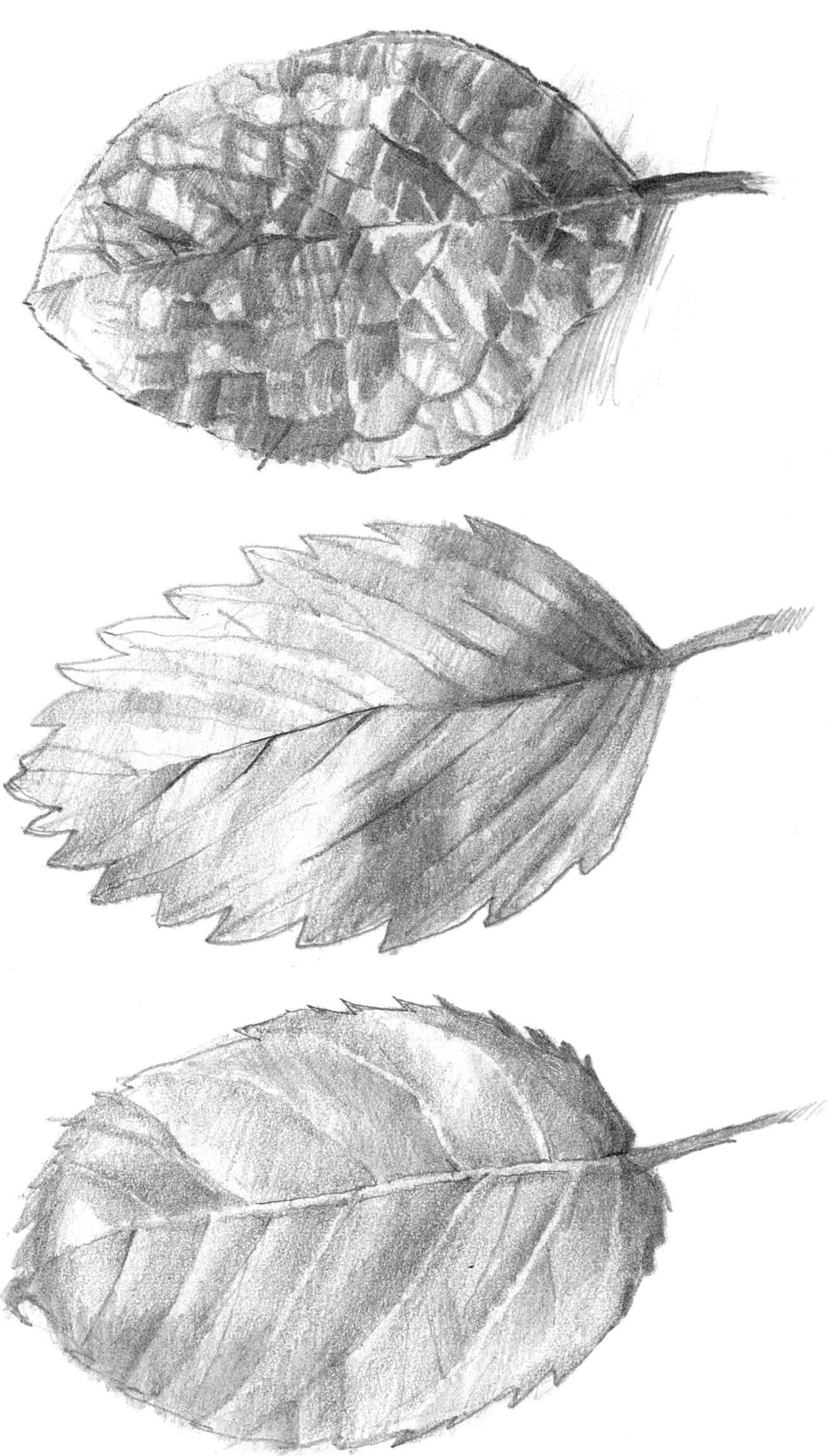

Patterns

Flowers lend themselves naturally to the creation of patterns and they have been an inspiration to designers and ornamentalists throughout history. Understanding how these patterns are evolved means learning to see flowerheads as if they were reduced to two dimensions.

The pansies I used for this oil painting were a common variety with splodges of colour in dark, geometric patterns. You could make a similar study with any flowers that have a strong design.

Look for the overall pattern, in this case a series of overlapping rings edged with another colour. Try to reproduce that while also showing the individual patterns within the flowerheads to give variety and interest.

Pansies are particularly useful because they come in many varieties that grow almost all year round, giving you something vivid to paint even when most of the garden is awash in winter rain and mud.

Try to find other flowers with the same sort of strong shapes. Variegated roses are splendid, but it is difficult to reduce their complicated structure to a simple outline.

Irises provide an interesting basic triple design, with opportunities for permutations in the different species – the simple flags of the woodland, and the Japanese varieties with their wide-open shapes. These flowers have long been translated into the famous fleurs-de-lis of the French royal house, and their name is also part of mythology. I love their tall, regal bearing, even though their season is so short. A good winter project is to see how many irises you can find in classical paintings, or Dutch still lives, textile designs, heraldic motifs, and so on.

If you have access to a photocopier, why not take the basic iris or pansy shape, and draw its outline on a template; then see how many unusual designs you can make, turning the flowerheads around, melding and matching shapes and colours.

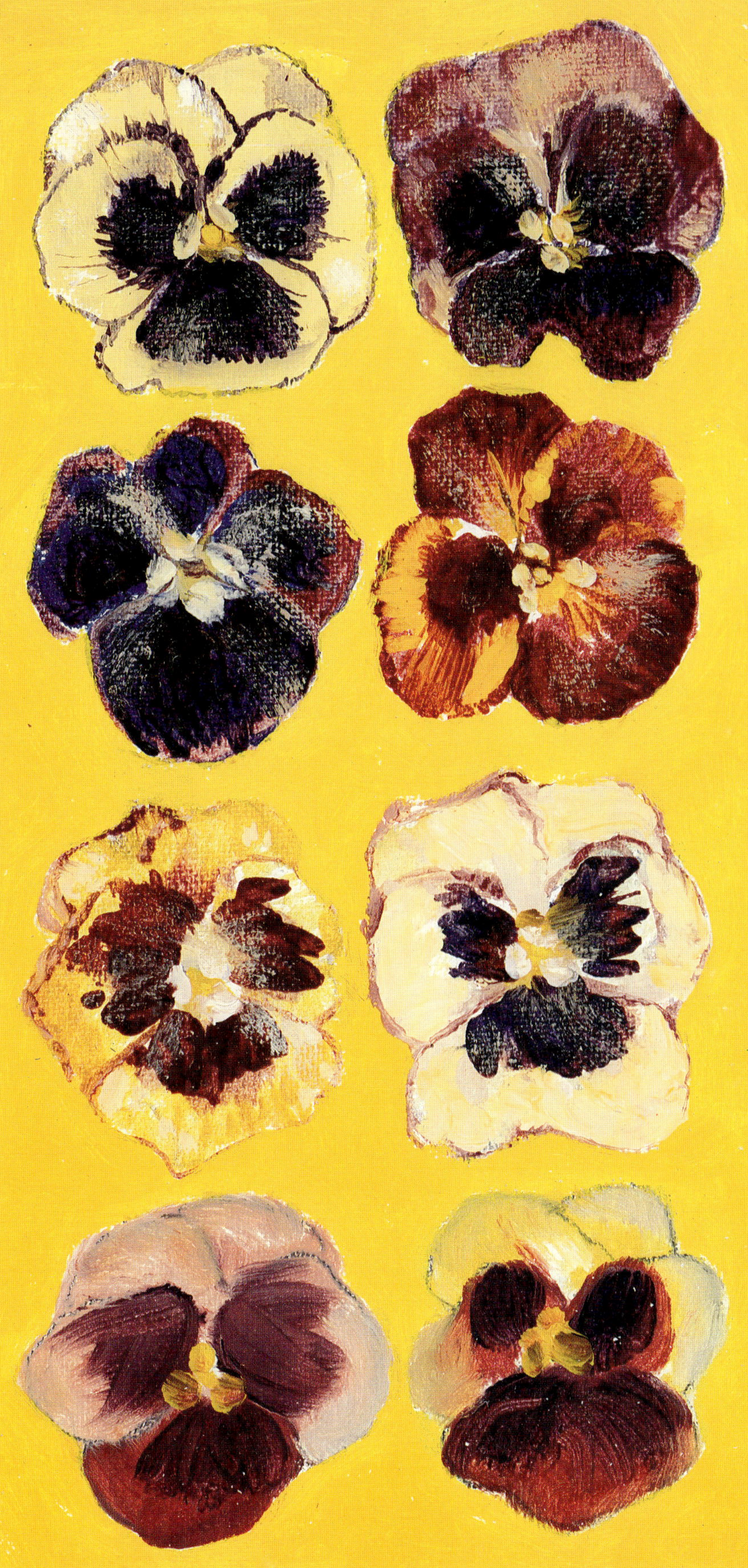

Special notes

On its own

Sometimes it's fun to paint a portrait of only one flower. Choose something that grows on a single stem, such as this daisy. The best way to see it clearly without picking it is to prop a piece of paper or a canvas board behind it to serve as a background.

A portrait of any kind is very different from a group painting; it gives the individual flower, like an individual person, an importance, a presence, which can be quite startling.

Choose a subject that takes this kind of spotlight well; this is one time to put aside most wild flowers, with their delicate stems and tiny multiple leaves. Find a brave single flower on a tall stem that you can make the focus of attention. The background in real life may well be green leaves, but I find it more effective if I wash in something else like this flat blue to create a curtain for my 'star'.

If you begin to work regularly with flowers, you'll find it worthwhile to make yourself a durable background prop that won't damage the plant or destroy nearby stems. Use two 3ft (1m) lengths of bamboo – either home-grown or canes from a garden store. Split them down from the top for about 2ft (60cm), which will give you enough area for a medium-sized plant. Slip a sheet of clean white paper between the canes, ideally watercolour paper, which is clear and bright without being shiny. Leave a good 2in (5cm) sticking out at either side to secure the paper; you could even tack it lightly to the bamboo. Finish by taping the canes around the top to close the slits.

Now you have a kind of screen. The bottom (unsplit) ends can be pushed into the ground on either side of your chosen flower, with the paper behind the stem, separating it from the rest. And when you have finished, you can pull it out, roll it up and take it home for your next outing.

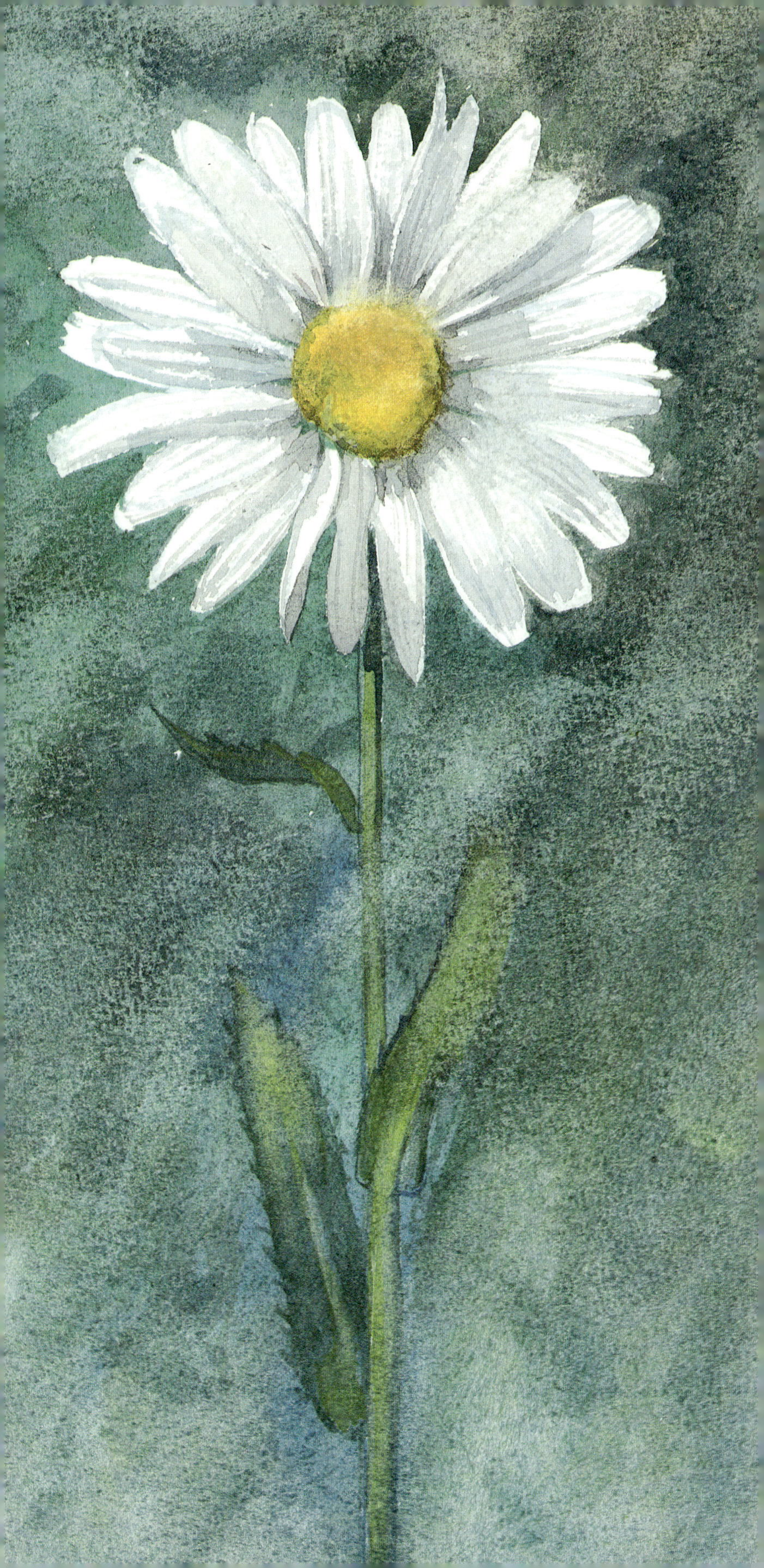

Relative values

An exciting way to intensify your appreciation of flowers is to make a study of one particular species. If you choose something rare enough to be hard to find, you give yourself a fine reason for travelling.

I have always been fascinated by orchids – both the cultivated varieties with their incredible array of showy flowers, and the wild orchids that still grow in fields, woodland and heath. Most of these areas are protected by law and fenced off from trespassers, so you need permission to paint there, but it is well worth the trouble.

This kind of study is much the same as the pencil studies of leaves on page 43. In both cases you are concentrating on individualized characteristics, comparing variety with variety. That is why I have put all the orchids on one page, even though they were painted miles apart, and on five different days.

This particular group is not very detailed. It was intended to give me the basic forms that I wanted to study, rather than the precise botanical features of each plant.

So often, I find that information gained from observation and experience has been absorbed without my being aware of it; because I find orchids really interesting, I can usually draw them quickly, noting the differences almost without looking at the sketch-pad.

But when I see a new flower, or one that I just don't enjoy looking at, I can labour over a drawing for hours and still produce something heavy, boring and totally unsatisfactory.

Of course, learning about a flower can help to change your whole approach. Many strange varieties are curious both in appearance and habit; you could find yourself intrigued by the appetite of Venus fly-traps, or the nocturnal exploits of night bloomers.

I suppose the answer is that we all have preferences – and it makes sense to try and work with them, instead of against them. It makes research fun, and provides another reason for your flower-hunting trips.

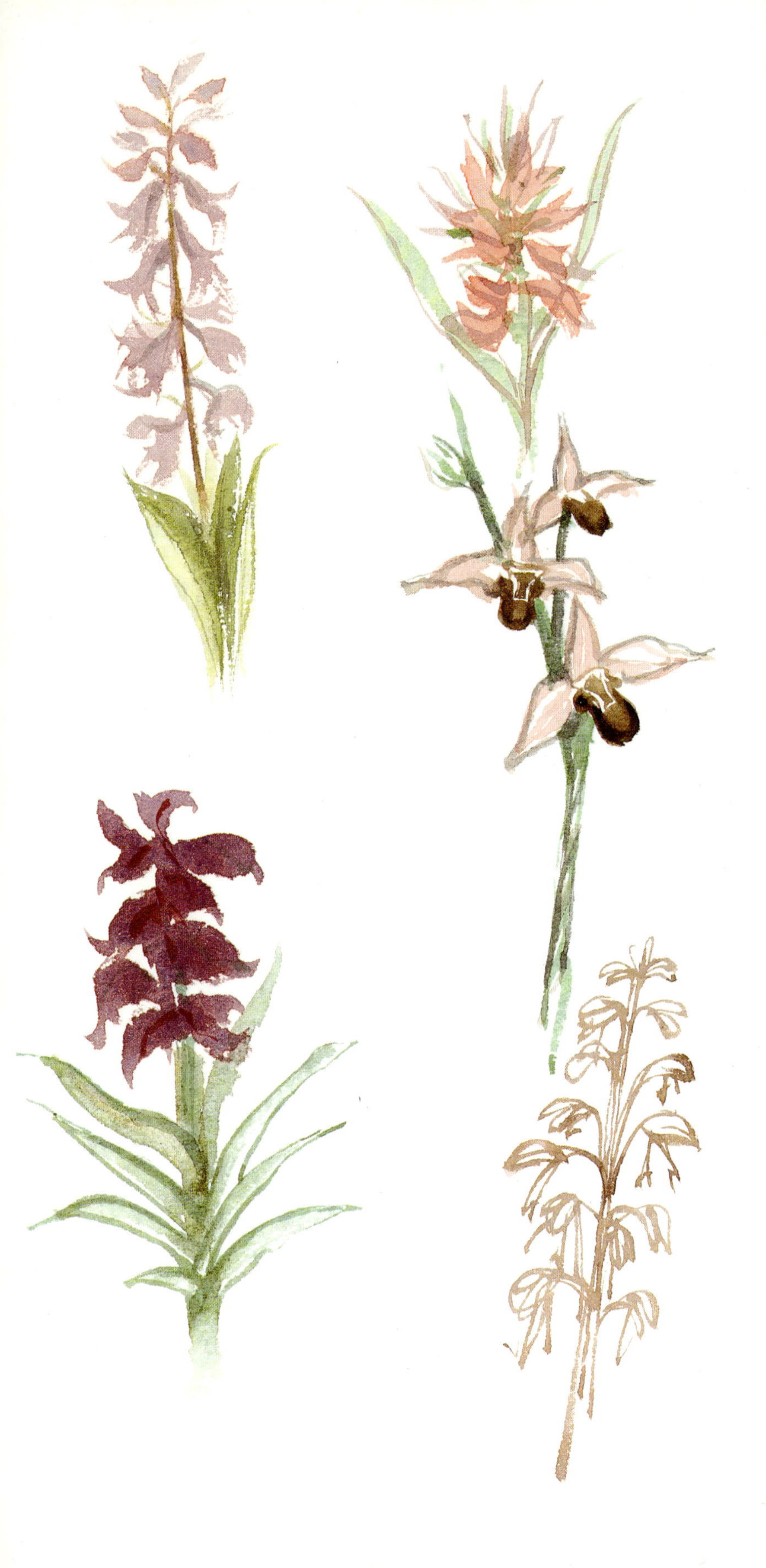

Background colours

One of the recurrent problems with flower-painting out of doors is the amount of green in the background. It often seems that everything is one particular shade of green. Yet when you get the painting home you see that the background is wrong – usually far darker than the green you remember seeing.

Although this is true of most outdoor painting, it is particularly annoying with flowers, because their colouring is so delicate that the wrong background can make the flower look completely wrong too.

When I did these clovers in midsummer, the grass was dark and rich, so I made the background dark. But at home it became obvious that the balance was all out of key. I could still see the meadow in my mind, and the entire effect was much brighter than the sketch in my studio.

So I quickly did another, using the same green made from viridian and black, with a great deal more turpentine in the mixture, to give the much lighter effect in the second example. Even though it was painted at home, the lighter green is far truer to the original than the first colour.

The greens of summer are extremely difficult to capture in paint. Before June, the bright new-leaf colours are easy, and the rich purples and reds of autumn seem to flow from the brush without any problems. But those mid-greens are really subtle and it may take a lot of experimenting before you find a palette that works for you.

As a general rule, even though you think you see the colours correctly, paint them four or five tones lighter and let the painting dry before you decide to add another darker tone. Outdoor flower painting must be fresh and bright, and it is always easier to add more colour than to take it away.

Don't be afraid, either, to experiment with colours. Although it is true that most flowers look natural against green or blue, you will find some interesting effects using other colours. Try dark blue or terracotta for white flowers (think how lovely climbing plants look against a brick wall) and grey stone tones for pinks and yellows.

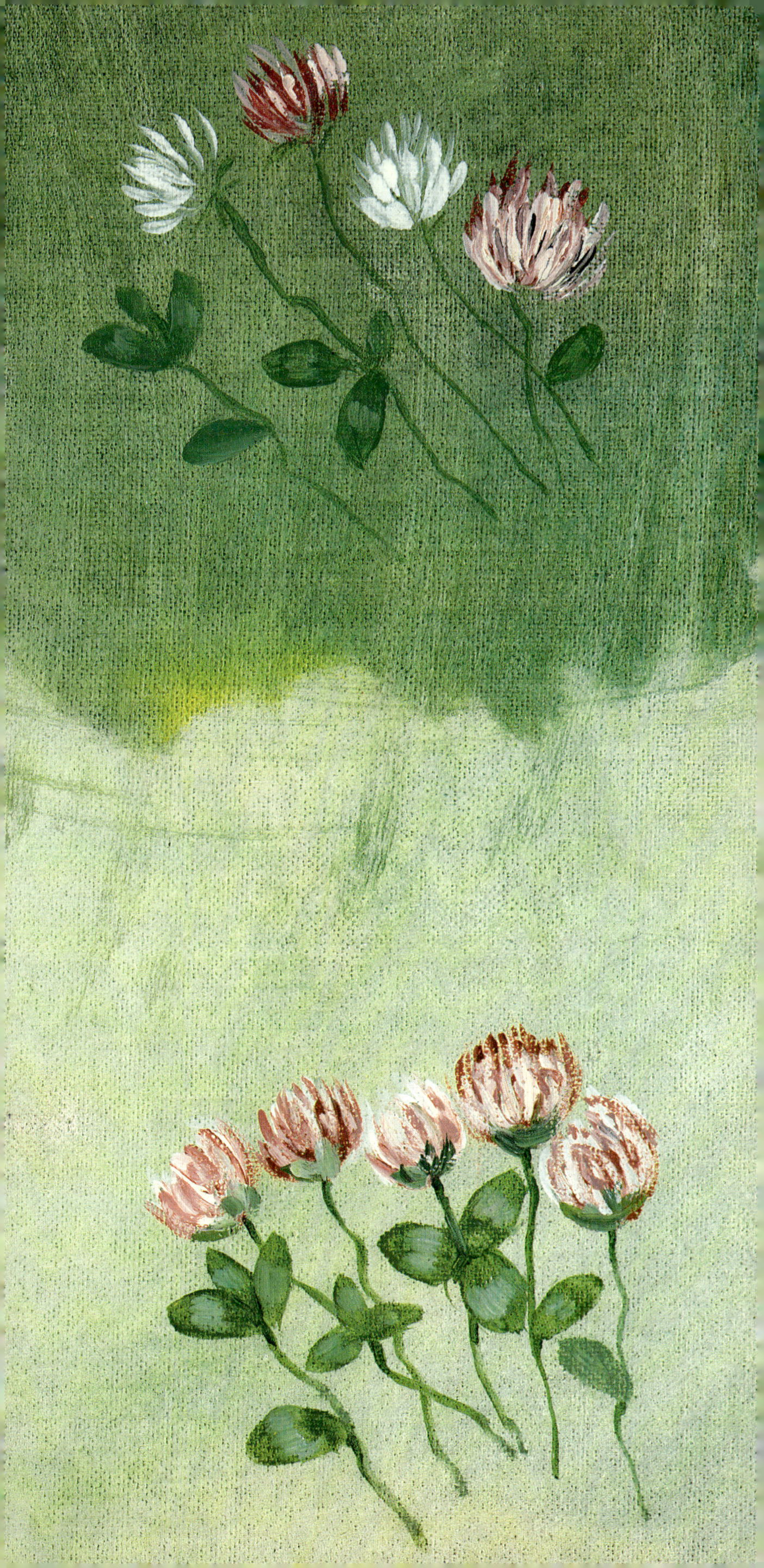

Working in tone

Although flower-painting could barely exist without all the colours of the rainbow, there are marvellous effects to be had by working in tones. Sometimes dead seed-pods show an incredible array; you can see at least five different siennas in this sketch of a poppy seed-head.

Tone painting can be greatly affected by the changing light. I use watercolour because it dries quickly in reasonable weather, allowing me to add each wash within five or six minutes. In watercolour you always work from light to dark. Put down the first wash in the palest tone you see, adding shadows and details in darker tones as you progress towards the front of the painting.

When you are in a hurry, paint with the paper flat rather than propped on an easel. The water soaks in evenly and dries evenly.

The leaves and flower-pods of the morning glory demonstrate a different kind of tone painting from that in the poppy. For the first, I used the loaded brush to create darker shadows in the same colour, made with one stroke. For the second, I used layers.

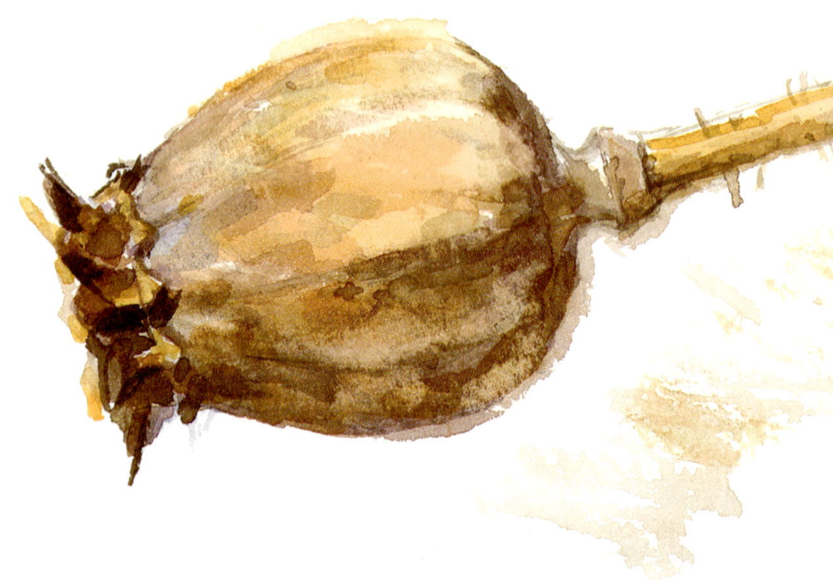

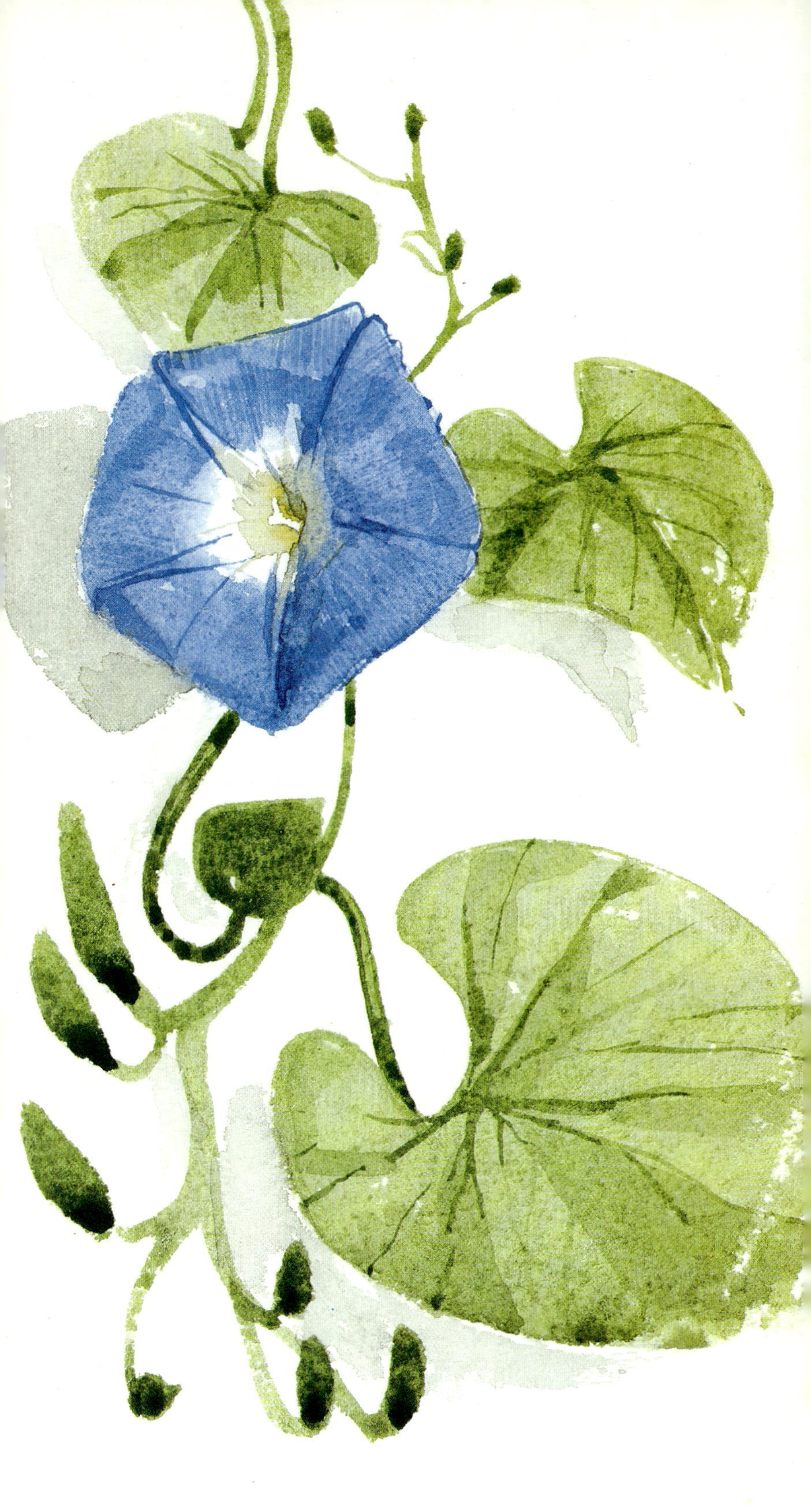

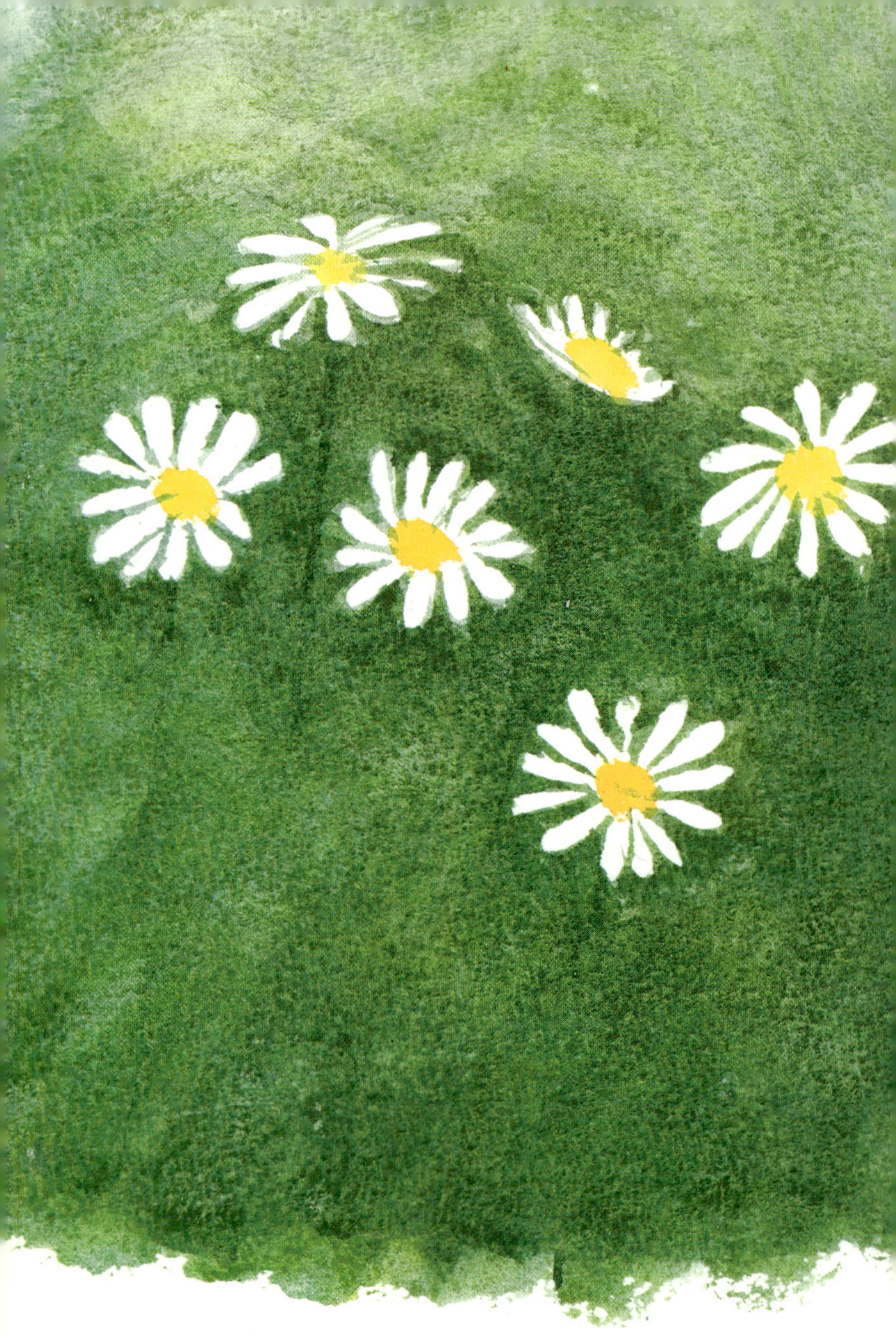

Working white

One of the astonishing things about painting is how much you can do with no colour at all. This is especially true of watercolour; you can play all kinds of tricks with white, and these examples use white in the two basic forms. Above, the

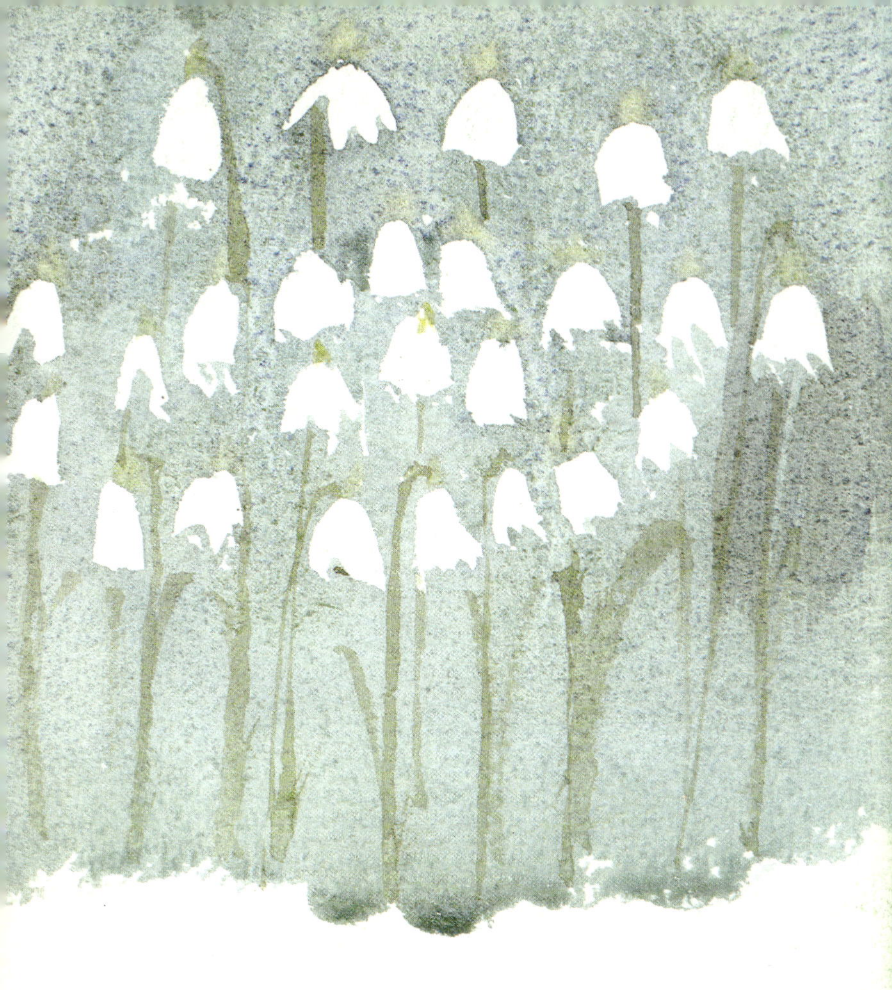

daisy petals have been outlined in light pencil under a green wash. Then they were painted over in chinese white. You only need a very little pigment.

The method used for the delicate snowdrops above was appropriately lighter. Using a watercolour resist liquid, I painted the flowerheads first before there was anything on the paper. After the resist dried, the pale turquoise wash went on in one broad action (you can see how it clotted a little at the base) and when that was half-dry, the stems were quickly lined in green. Then the whole sketch was allowed to become really dry, the resist was gently rubbed off with my fingertips, and the painting was finished. In all, a matter of fifteen minutes or so. Resist liquid, which smells absolutely awful, is nonetheless a very useful tool, letting you make lovely smooth washes right over any kind of shape. You might call it negative painting.

A first approach: the flower album

When you first begin to look at flowers, it is astonishing to realize how many ideas and designs are based on their shapes and colours. Undoubtedly they are chosen also for their more subtle association with beautiful things, and for the natural harmony we find in their presence.

So there are flowers on our fabrics, china, embroidery, furniture, sofa cushions, brilliantly printed wallpaper. There are flower shapes in architecture – on ornamental metalwork, on iron gates and on monochrome woodwork.

Make an album by painting or drawing every flower you can see from your chair at home. Put several on each sheet instead of doing them singly. This will remind your eye of the tiny changes in detail that are so important when you work on a small scale.

You can make a diary of flower images, noting down the sources of your illustrations, and keeping colour notes as well. It is fascinating to see how artists and designers change nature's colours, and even more fascinating to see what they put in their place.

Our brains sometimes limit the changes we will accept; a purple daffodil might be a new horticultural creation, but few people would accept it without question in a naturalistic painting. On the other hand, working out the originals of the flowers entwined in a William Morris wallpaper is a lesson in creativity; white lilies become dark green, blue or red.

When you find interesting wallpapers, try and get samples of the various colourways; most manufacturers will send these free of charge. Look at them individually and then compare them. Which colour pattern do you prefer, and why?

Trying out new combinations of blending and contrasting flower shapes can inspire you to experiment with your own drawings, ringing the changes in colour and medium. Pin your album pages up where they are easily visible; like the information on a frieze or a wall chart, the results of your experiments will be digested gradually, almost without you being aware of it.

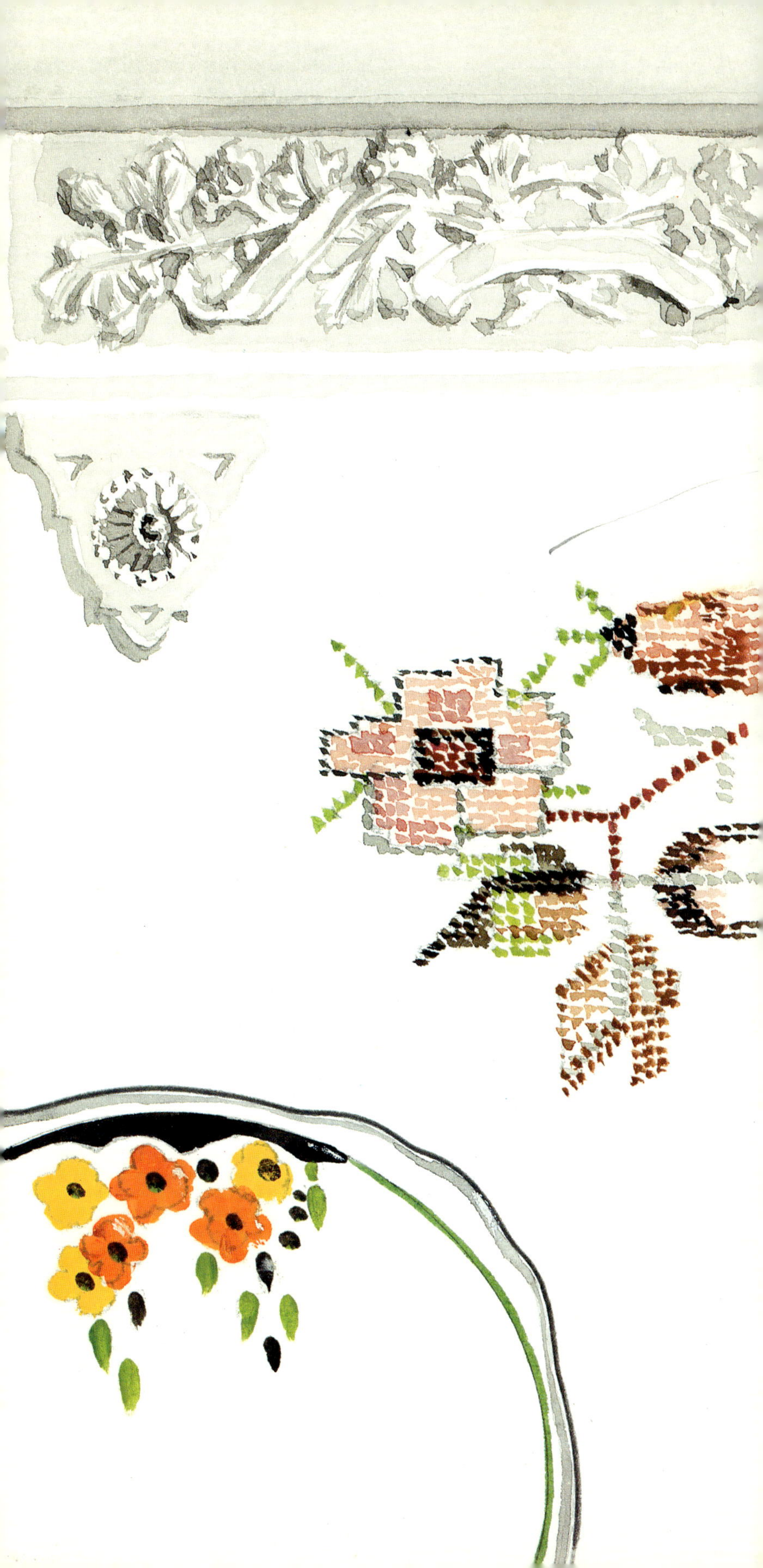

A second approach: double helpings

After working on a small scale, it is valuable to find ways of creating larger-than-life effects, even in a small notebook.

Sunflowers are a spectacular subject for this purpose. They have been a favourite of many painters such as Van Gogh, whose still life of a vase of sunflowers is one of the most popular prints ever sold.

Studying great paintings – his, and those of other artists – can be a revelation. Van Gogh painted sunflowers over and over again, and most of his studies are made up of the simplest brush-strokes in two colours, yellow and ochre. Only thick paint, brush marks and a few, a very few, details, and the painting is incredibly effective.

Here is an enjoyable way of trying out your own sunflower on a grand scale. I painted only half the flowerhead, in order to get it on to the page in something like the right proportion to reality. If you hold the page at right angles to a mirror, you'll see the whole bloom. This can work well with any symmetrical flower – a large peony, for example, or a rose. But it is not quite so effective with flowers whose heads hang, like fuchsias or daffodils.

Working in halves like this will also demonstrate how unsymmetrical most flowers really are. Try painting a whole sunflower exactly the same size as the half, and holding it above the image in the mirror. You'll probably find that the mirror flower looks more natural than the whole one. Because we expect to see symmetry, we think it exists even when brief examination would show how much variety there is in this – or any – flowerhead.

An enjoyable extra project is to find a flower at your local garden show which has been bred precisely for exact symmetry; some rose and dahlia breeders concetrate on this particular feature. I think you'll find that once you have learned to look carefully, if you paint such a flower exactly as it is, it will look false.

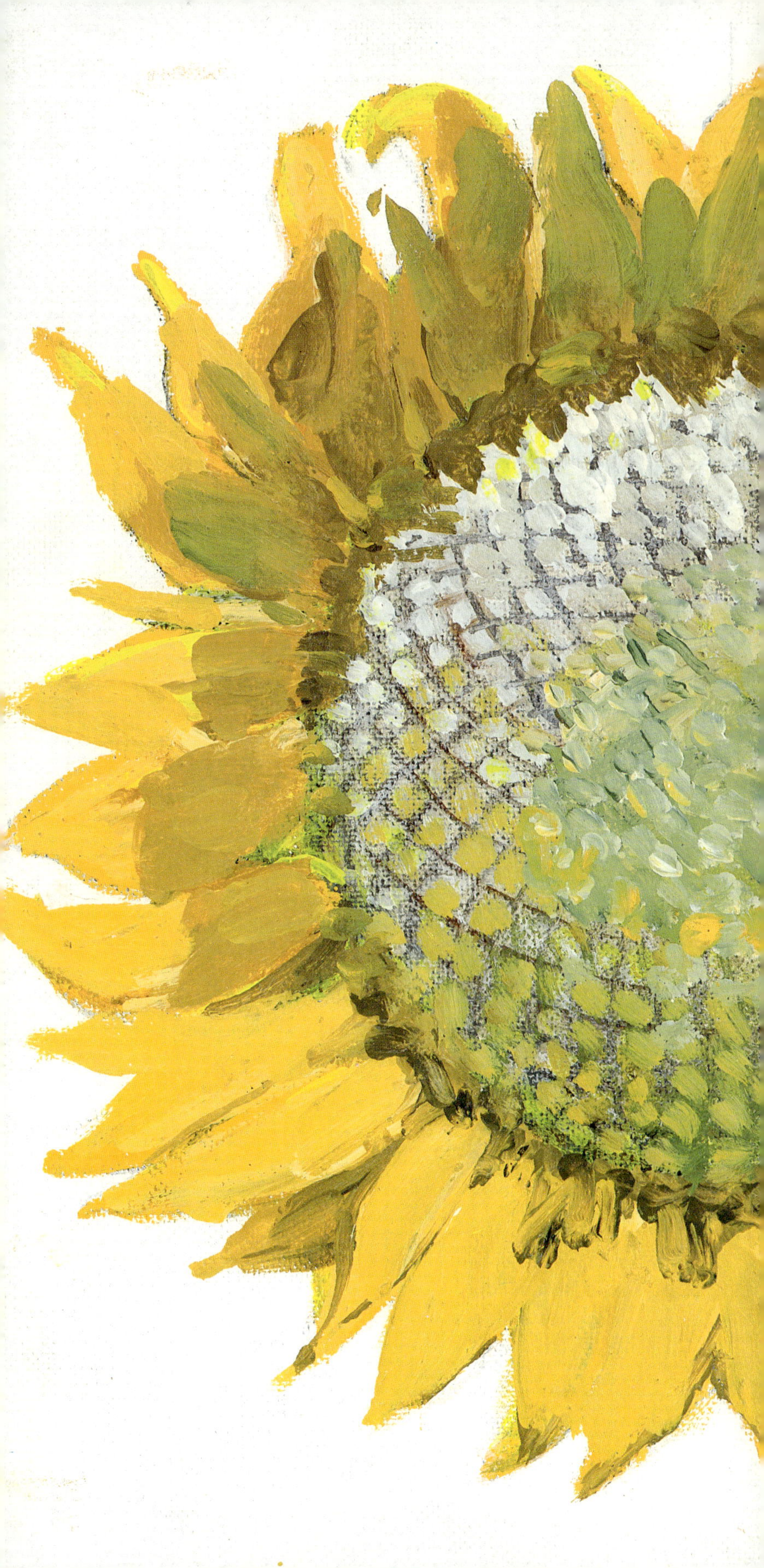

A final challenge: botanical accuracy

Botanical painting is entirely unique, almost a separate art-form, with its detailed analysis of every part of the plant. It pays particular attention to the botanical structures that are used in classifying the flower according to genus, family and species – an art devoted to the service of extended knowledge. Today many illustrators try to combine precise observation with the more decorative effect of flower painting.

It is very good training for any artist to try and convey something of the quality of botanical study even at the most basic level. This drawing of a yellow flag with its strongly marked leaves is in the spirit of that tradition.

Before you begin work, you will have to dig up the plant, so choose a common variety. Clean off the root growth carefully, and lay the plant beside your drawing-pad. Don't rush your work. Make sketches and drawings first, noting any startling features which you will be able to emphasize.

Plan the final drawing so that it fills the page, but leave enough space for additional details; if there are interesting leaves, or an unusual flower bud, you might try a close-up in a circle. The intention of a botanical drawing is primarily to convey information, but it is still a demanding art form, and the finished work should look as satisfying as possible.

The more you draw impressionistically, the more important it is to develop the control of eye and hand that botanical drawing will give you. Keep your studies and add to them regularly.

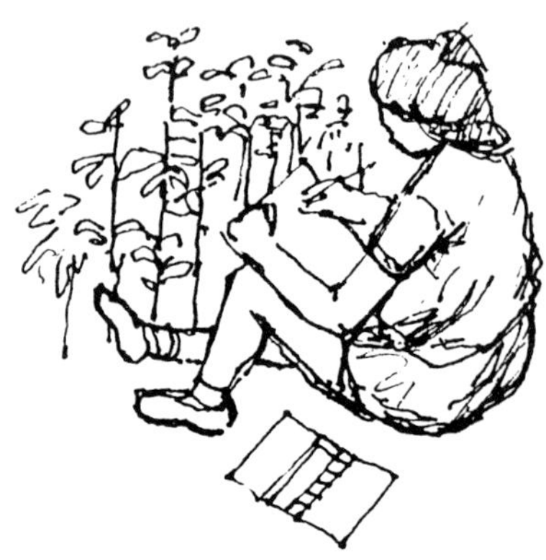

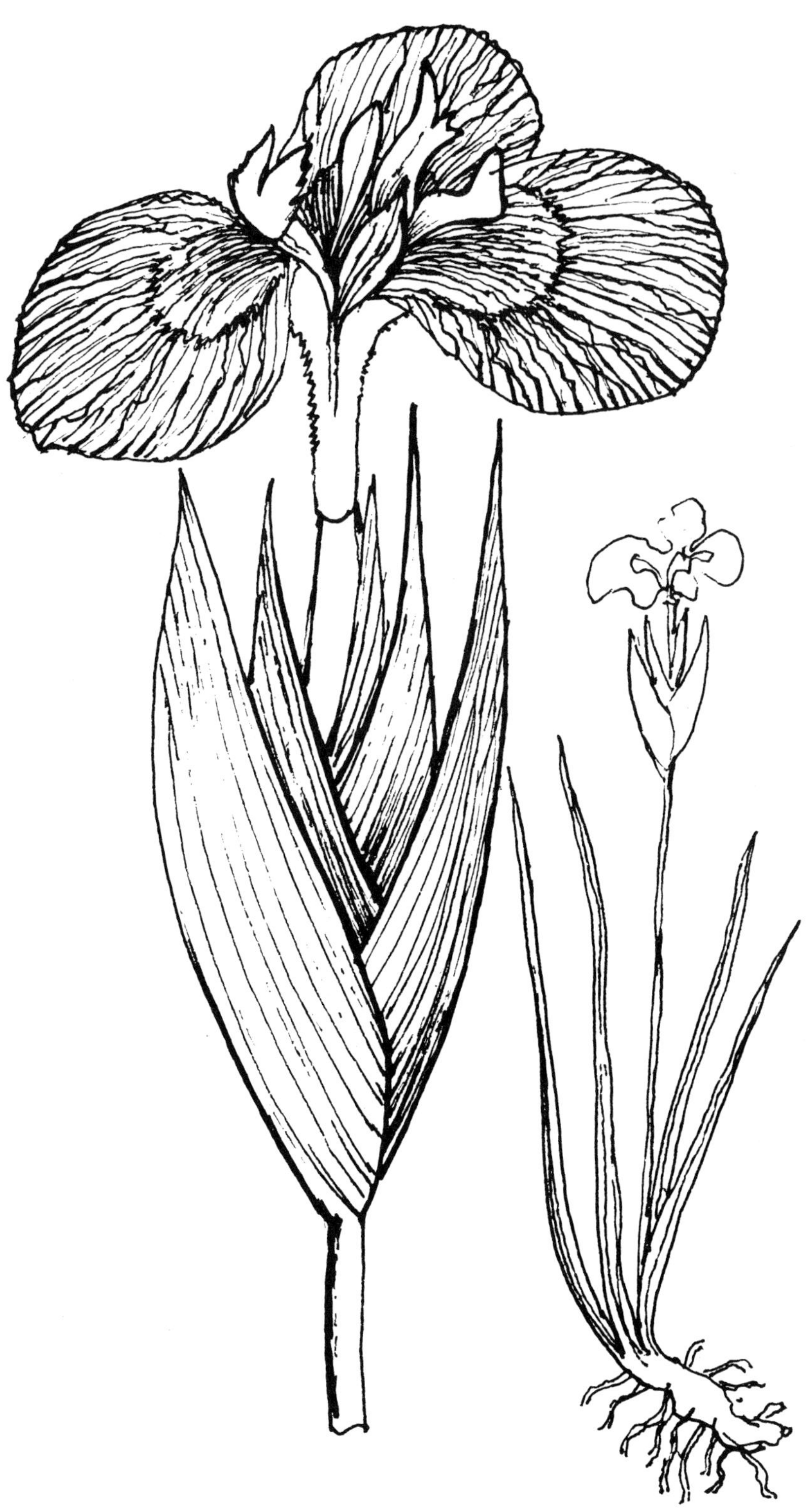

Going home

A flower painter usually carries a light load, so it is tempting to take a collection of wild flowers home, and keep on painting. Remember, though, that there are legal penalties for picking anything except common weeds.

A daisy, buttercup or wild herb can be as beautiful as any native orchid, so here are two aids to taking them home. The box, lined in plastic and filled with compost, holds rooted plants; the cardboard, with loose rubber bands, will keep a spray or two safely upright and protected.

When you arrive home, put the flowers in water or set them out to dry while you think about what you have accomplished. Be fairly critical so that you gain from the experience. If a rose looks lovely, but the stems are angular and too stiff, concentrate on stems and shrubs the next time out. If leaves and stems bend gracefully, but the flowers look clumsy and heavy, make a number of studies just of the blossom. If the colours look too heavy, make a note to use a lighter touch the next time, and bring the painting home to compare it with the earlier one.

Learning to be a painter is a job for life. Every small accomplishment will bring you a little nearer your goal – even though you set yourself higher standards. No one ever said it would be easy. But it will be infinitely satisfying.

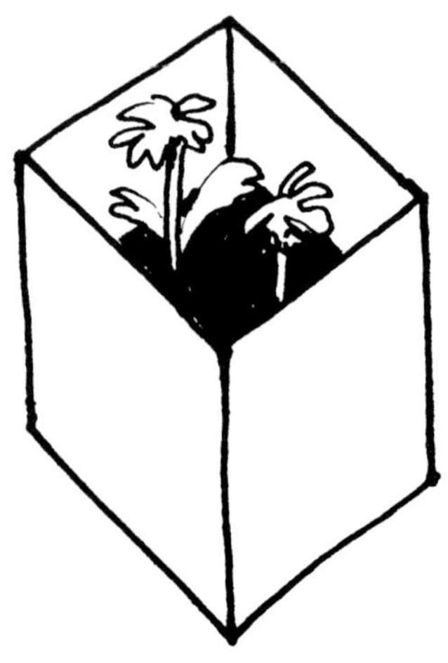

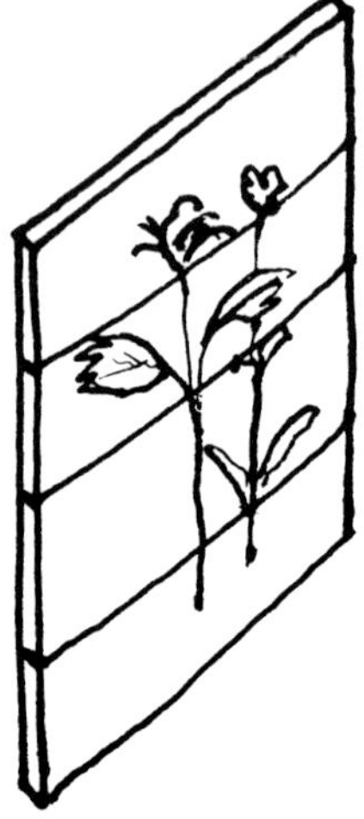

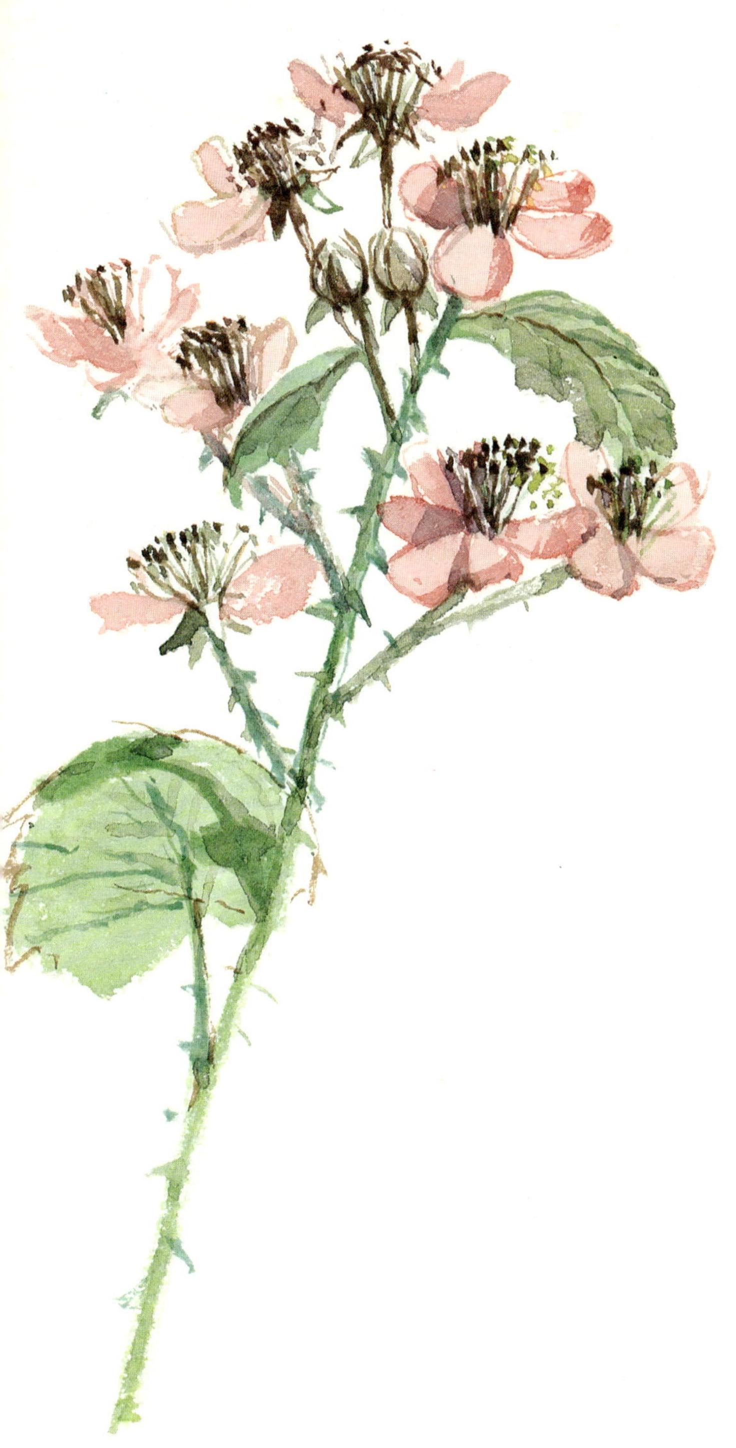

Index

Page numbers in *italic* refer to captions and illustrations.

Note on colour charts: the guides in this book have been produced within the limitations of four-colour process printing, and therefore cannot reflect the intensity of certain pure pigments.